The
ASSERTIVENESS
Workbook

Dena Michelli

To Ben, Verity, Rosie, Zoë-Hope, Michael and Oscar, with love.

Teach Yourself®

The ASSERTIVENESS Workbook

Dena Michelli

Meet the author

Dena Michelli has enjoyed two main careers. She started life as a mechanical engineer where she learned to make and move physical systems. She is now a leadership coach where she informs and influences human systems.

As a researcher and author, Dena aims to help people to build self-awareness so they can make informed choices about how they express themselves and determine what impact they wish to have on others. By showing people how to make use of the myriad tools that exist to enhance their communication skills, she enables them to take charge of their lives and successes, and to live wholeheartedly according to their innate talents and aspirations.

Dena graduated with a PhD from the University of Surrey, where she identified the processes that people experience as they move through personal transformation. This informs her work and enables her to encourage individuals to challenge themselves, to tap into their capabilities and to achieve goals that they may have thought were beyond their reach.

As an aside, she designs and makes stained glass windows and has recently graduated from Swansea Metropolitan University with an MA in Architectural Glass.

Acknowledgements

In writing this book, I have many to thank. The circle that is my family, all three generations of it and all extensions of it, has been a collective guinea pig as I explored self-assertion. I must thank them all for their indulgence and tolerance as I careened from one communication experiment to another.

My friends, some of whom have mastered and model assertion beautifully, have been an inspiration. I often ask myself what they would do if they were in my shoes and feed on the answer.

My colleagues, all of whom exemplify the qualities that have informed this workbook. Each is incalculably supportive and gracious. I have been taught, held and nurtured by you all.

I value all of you for your perspicacity in identifying the rich territory on which assertiveness may be explored and the accumulation of wisdom you shared so willingly. As always, you come up with something unusual yet pertinent and combine it with a pragmatic view on the topic. This is, indeed, a collective effort.

Thank you.

Contents

How to use this workbook

In this chapter you will learn:
- ▶ *the definition of assertiveness*
- ▶ *what prevents you from being assertive*
- ▶ *the learning stages that you will go through to develop a new skill*
- ▶ *your learning preference – how you naturally approach your learning*
- ▶ *how to use the workbook to capture your learning*

→ Welcome to *The Assertiveness Workbook*!

By picking up this book and working your way through it, you're on the way to becoming more assertive and able to take charge of your life. Indeed, in itself, it was an assertive act!

By deciding to address your assertiveness skills, you're also putting yourself on a continual path of self-development. Stepping into the world of assertiveness sets up a whole series of knock-on effects that will present you with new challenges, new awareness and an increasing level of self-assurance. Not only this, but also you'll be able to make your choices with a clear head. No longer will you be awash with those old, diminishing, messages that seep into your mind from your past, but you'll have clarity around 'what's yours' and 'what's not yours' in terms of the psychological and emotional baggage that you're carrying.

Speaking of 'baggage', the term 'assertiveness' carries quite a lot of baggage of its own. Coined in the seventies, and reaching its ascendancy in the eighties and nineties, assertiveness heralded the notion of 'rights' in communication. Such as:

▶ 'I have a right to be heard.'

▶ 'I have a right to ask for what I need.'

▶ 'I have a right to make my own choices.'

▶ 'I have a right to say "No!"'

Although these 'rights' are undeniably true, they gathered such social momentum that those who adopted an 'assertive' style of communication began to be confused with those who were 'aggressive'. This led to assertive people being considered 'scary', 'dominant' or 'ballsy' – particularly if they were female! So, to normalize the definition of assertiveness, it is not about trespassing on others' wishes, nor is it about getting what you want all the time.

'Assertiveness is about making choices about what and how you communicate whilst representing yourself honestly and authentically. It is also about recognizing yours and others' rights in negotiating the outcome of your conversation.'

When you consider the wider situation in which your communication takes place, being assertive may mean taking a more dominant or recessive role in conveying your message so that the desired outcome, in the long term, may be achieved. The point is, the tools of assertiveness may be used, or not, depending on your best judgement of what will serve you and your counterpart in the end.

Let's look at the mechanics of assertiveness...

→ What stops you from being assertive?

Although a definition of assertiveness has been given above, it does not reveal the underlying structure of assertive communication, nor does it reveal the motivations behind individuals' communication style. Rather, it is more the visible end of assertiveness; it describes what assertiveness *is*. It would be wonderful if you could short-circuit the hard work and just adopt the assertive style, but it is not everyone's gift to be able to do this. Most of us need to understand how our strings are pulled and how we can take back the control that, in fact, belonged to us in the first place.

If you think back to your formative years, you'll probably recall your parental injunctions as you first tried to assert yourself on the world. Which ones resonate with you ...?

▶ Don't be selfish!

▶ Share your toys nicely!

▶ Who do you think you are to push in front of others?

▶ Don't interrupt!

▶ Don't show off!

▶ Only speak when you're spoken to!

▶ Let others have a go first!

▶ _____

▶ _____

▶ _____

Add some of your own.

Have a think about what your childhood messages were from your parents and what effect they have had on your communication style. Then think about what you'd like to replace these messages with. You can use the table below to capture some of these. (You'll find a worked example taken from the list above to help you on your way.)

Think about your parental injunctions and write them down below	Think about the effect that this injunction has on your communication	What would you like to replace your parental message with?
Don't be selfish, put others first!	*This puts me on the back foot and, when I habitually put others first, I often fail to get my needs met.*	*Getting my needs met does not mean I'm selfish.*

Once you've identified those phrases that hijack your communication capability and render you a child again, you can begin to change the content and power of them. Indeed, you have already started to do this by bringing them to mind and making yourself aware of them and the effect they have upon you.

Exercise 1

Try observing yourself when you're communicating and see if you can catch yourself falling into one of these old communication patterns. (If you feel unable to do this, ask someone who knows you well to point them out to you – kindly. This will help you identify the sort of occasion that triggers your pattern and you will be able to 'tune in' and observe yourself at those times.)

Bringing a behaviour or tendency to awareness is the first step towards making the changes we desire. If we are 'out of awareness', we just keep on doing what we've always done. If we are 'in awareness', we have a choice to continue doing what we've always done, or change it.

This makes it all sound very simple. However, being aware of our susceptibilities is not the only thing that is needed to make the changes we wish; it is just the first step. The second step is to decide how we're going to stop ourselves from falling into our old habits, and what we're going to replace them with. Thirdly, we need to develop the skills to get the results we want – and then we need to practise them until they feel natural to us. This process is often described as 'the learning ladder'.

→ The Learning Ladder

The Learning Ladder is a way of conceiving the challenges of learning something new. Think of learning to drive a car.

1 To begin with, you are unaware of what you don't know; you are *unconsciously incompetent*.

2 Then, your driving instructor takes pains to explain to you all the skills you need to perfect in order to drive safely. 'Mirror, signal, manoeuvre!' (Whilst disengaging the clutch, changing gear, re-engaging the clutch and moving forward more slowly or more quickly, depending on the traffic conditions, which you must appraise and respond to appropriately.) When you first try to do this, it's a bit 'hit and miss' and you may find yourself leaving out one of the steps. It may also feel somewhat unnatural to you. This stage is called *consciously incompetent*. Now you *know* what you don't know!

3 As you practise combining these activities, you become more and more adept and you begin to feel confident that you're making progress. However, you are still very conscious of each step and concentrate hard to get them in the correct order and properly completed. You are now *consciously competent*.

4 Finally, as you become familiar with the sequence of skills that are demanded of an able driver, it begins to feel quite normal. It is almost as if the controls are a natural extension of your body, and you notice that you're driving 'out of consciousness'. (This is not the same as driving without thinking!) Indeed, experienced drivers often reach their destination without recalling any of the driving! This stage is called *unconscious competence*. You are in your flow.

Forgetting driving for a moment, learning a new mode of communication offers a similar set of challenges. To begin with, you may be unaware of the pitfalls in your communication style (*unconscious incompetence*). When you observe yourself, or someone else gives you feedback, you begin to be aware of your errors and the full extent of your challenge becomes apparent (*conscious incompetence*). Then you try out new things and sometimes they work, but sometimes they don't (*conscious competence*). Eventually, your new and much more effective communication style becomes a habit and it disappears from consciousness until further refinement is required (*unconscious competence*).

This is how it looks:

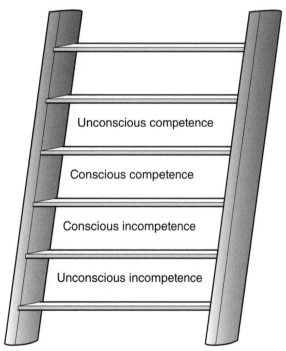

Unconscious competence

Conscious competence

Conscious incompetence

Unconscious incompetence

The Learning Ladder

So, how are you going to keep yourself going up the ladder and prevent yourself from losing your footing?

Here are some ways you might consider for supporting yourself through your learning. Add some of your own at the bottom of the list.

► Find a supportive friend to give you feedback and encourage you.

► Create a vision of what life will be like when you're confidently assertive and find a representative image or metaphor to pin on the wall.

► If your current communication style has held you back from doing something you love, set a goal to pursue it.

► Put yourself in situations that call for assertive communication.

► _____

_____

► _____

_____

► _____

_____

→ Learning preferences – what is your learning style?

We all have different preferences for the way we learn new things. By being aware of this, you can plan your learning according to your natural inclinations, thereby enhancing your ability to succeed.

The theories of adult learning suggest that people show one of four main preferences when they begin their learning journey. This preference may be consistently chosen – an intrinsic preference – or it may vary depending upon the situation that calls for learning – an extrinsic preference. Once they get going, however, they may then move to a secondary or supportive preference to deepen their learning. The four preferences are:

▶ learning by 'doing'

▶ learning by observing and 'reflecting'

▶ learning by thinking and 'building a theory'

▶ learning by trying things out and 'experimenting'.

To show the relationship between one preference and another, these four learning preferences are often expressed as a cycle. The idea behind this is that once the cycle has been entered, effective learning is achieved by passing through the subsequent preferences in sequence.

For instance:

▶ Firstly, you have an experience by 'doing' something.

▶ Then you 'reflect' on that experience.

▶ Next, you 'build a theory' about that experience.

▶ Then you 'experiment' or try it out in reality.

Starting again (or deepening your present learning), you have another experience...

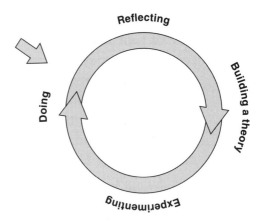

Learning preferences cycle

The diagram above shows someone entering the cycle with a 'doing' preference. (Someone else might prefer to 'reflect' on something before they 'build a theory', entering the cycle at the 'reflecting' position. Or they may prefer to 'build a theory' before 'experimenting'. Or 'experiment' before trying out something new.)

This adult learning theory was derived from Kolb by Honey and Mumford.

You may like to reflect on your preferred style of learning. Think of your peak learning moments. How did the learning occur to you?

▶ What style did you adopt during your peak learning experience?

▶ How did you feel about sitting in a classroom compared to getting things done?

▶ What did your teachers say about your learning approach?

▶ What types of learning experiences have been uncomfortable for you?

▶ When has your learning been most enjoyable? Why?

Exercise 2

Use the table below to fill in the details of your learning and notice if the 'Hows' have a similar theme or if they differ from one situation to another. There is a worked example below to get you going.

What have been my peak learning experiences?	How did I learn the lessons?
Learning to give presentations has been one of the most confidence boosting activities I've ever done.	I learned to do this by being thrown in at the deep end and having to make a presentation at short notice. I didn't have time to prepare so I just stood up and talked for half an hour – thankfully, about something I knew lots about! There were 50 people in the audience and once I started, I just found my voice and it flowed from there. Now, I'm happy to give presentations.
1	
2	
3	

The example above suggests that this person learned from 'doing' in this instance. It is valuable to note this preference because 'doing' may suggest the best way for this person to learn other things – or, the best way to start learning about other things.

By being conscious of your learning style, you will be able to develop your assertiveness skills in the most favourable way for you.

<hr>

→ Using this workbook

This workbook has been designed to meet the needs of all readers by offering activities, ideas, concepts and theories. So, whatever your preferred learning approach is, there should be an exercise or activity to help you get going.

It is probably helpful to read the first few chapters first. It will be these that hold the basics of assertiveness and it will be these that build the foundation stone upon which the more specific examples will be built. As the workbook progresses, increasingly difficult assertiveness topics will be presented; those that are notoriously tricky to deal with. Once the early chapters are digested, you can pick and choose the chapters that are most relevant to you.

Some of you will not want to work through the exercises because understanding the concept is enough. Others of you will not particularly want to reflect on your experiences because you prefer to stockpile practical tools and techniques. However, a thorough examination of the material in your chosen chapters is recommended. It really will build your knowledge of the subject along with your skills. These two attributes, cognitive and behavioural, form an essential partnership that will ensure you meet your assertiveness challenges with increasing capability. Theory without practice doesn't change people's experience of your behaviour. Practice without theory merely perpetuates your current behaviour.

Even if you consider yourself to be naturally assertive, enter this workbook with an open mind and explore the territory with curiosity. By working through the exercises, you will see your skills in a new light and be more conscious of the impact you have on others. It is always possible that what you believe to be assertive may be perceived as something else by the recipients of your messages. It is worth checking this out, therefore, and bringing greater awareness to your approach.

Make this a working document. Highlight those things that strike you as relevant. Fill in the questionnaires and use the tick boxes to keep track of your views and feelings. Write in the margins and make comments that will help you capture and retain your learning.

Otherwise, keep a journal of your thoughts, insights, experiences, feedback and progress. In this way, you can get a real sense of what works for you and what doesn't. There are two templates below that may help you. One is more like a journal and the other is more like an action plan. If you prefer a different format, think about how you'd like to capture your experiences, record your successes and keep your nose to the grindstone. Perhaps a video diary would be more suitable for you. Or, you may prefer to create a spreadsheet for yourself – or make a project plan. You may also consider getting yourself a coach; someone who is 'on your side' and prepared to listen to you as you reflect on and digest the results of your practice. We all have different ways of making sense of our learning journeys so pick one that works for you.

Learning journal – keeping a note

What are my insights, inspirations, realizations, thoughts, concerns, hopes….?	
Remaining 'true to myself', what skill or capability would I like to develop?	
What will 'success' look like, in what context will it be experienced and how will I feel about that?	
What are my next steps and when will I take them?	

Action plan – deciding what to do

Date:

Desired outcome: *(This will be one step that will get you closer to your overarching goal)*
A worked example is shown in italics.
1 I'd like to make a contribution during my next departmental meeting.

My planned action: *(This is the specific action that you aim to take)*
1 I will look at the agenda beforehand and identify a topic on which I have something to say.
2 I'll gather the relevant information and prepare my thinking so that I am ready to make my point.
3 I will rehearse this with my coach so that I am familiar with the sound of my voice speaking the words I want to say.

Key observations/insights/learning points:
1 I felt very nervous waiting for the moment to arrive. My mouth was dry and I didn't have any water to hand.
2 I made my point and it seemed to be well received. In fact, the chairperson commented on its usefulness.
3 I felt really pleased with myself and thought that I could do this again.

Feedback: *(This can be requested from anyone that you trust who was present and witnessed your action.)*
1 I asked my colleague for feedback.
2 She said that I had been clear in making my point and that I was well spoken.
3 She also said that I could have looked people in the eye rather than looking down at my papers.
4 She also said that my body language was not strong; that I was crouched. This looked weak.

Next steps:
1 I'm going to practise sitting upright and looking people in the eye when I speak to them.
2 I'd like to learn more about body language.
3 I'm also going to look for another opportunity to make a contribution in a meeting.

The consequences to me of my new skill:
1 I'll feel more confident speaking in groups.
2 I'll be able to take on more responsibilities and volunteer for projects.
3 It will impact my personal life inasmuch as I'll be able to make bolder choices.

However you decide to plot your route to a confident assertive style, whether it be this book replete with annotations or a learning journal in some form, it will measure your progress from where you were when you first picked up this book to where you got to when you last put it down. The difference is worth noting and celebrating!

Summary

This chapter was concerned with ensuring that you are equipped with sufficient understanding of your learning style to benefit your learning plan. Having worked through the exercises, you should have a fair idea of how you like to approach your learning. You can use this knowledge to pick from the variety of exercises and choose those that will be most effective in propelling you towards an assertive style of communication.

Where to next?

The next chapter is going to focus on finding out where you are in the communication stakes. This diagnosis will furnish you with the information you need to get started. By holding a realistic view of what your communication skills are like, you will be able to set off in the right direction towards your ultimate goal.

So, enjoy getting into the subject of assertiveness and allow it to enable and enhance your life, your relationships and your self-confidence.

What have I learnt?

➔ Using the definition of assertiveness, how do I view my dominant communication style?

_____

_____

_____

_____

_____

_____

_____

➔ What have I learnt about my learning style as a result of reading this chapter?

_____

_____

_____

_____

_____

_____

_____

→How can I help myself learn more effectively?

_____

_____

_____

_____

_____

_____

_____

_____

→Who do I trust to mentor me during my learning?

_____

_____

_____

_____

_____

_____

_____

_____

2 What type of communication style do you tend to use?

In this chapter you will learn:
- ▶ *what your natural communication style is*
- ▶ *how assertive you are*
- ▶ *what happens to your communication style when you're stressed*
- ▶ *the mindset, or basic belief about yourself, that drives your communication*
- ▶ *what your communication goal is.*

This is the beginning of your journey towards taking command of your communication. Once confident that you can choose how to respond to the situations you encounter, you'll be able to take responsibility for their outcome and enjoy your successes.

Firstly, it's important to identify your communication style. We often have fantasies about how we communicate, some overly flattering, some unrealistically poor.

This chapter is going to focus on getting the diagnosis correct. By being clear about where you're starting from, you'll be able to plot your route to your desired outcome.

Firstly, you will be asked to make a 'guesstimate' of how satisfied you are with your communication style and the outcomes you get.

Secondly, you will be asked to answer a series of questions that will help you identify the level of your assertiveness.

Finally, you will be encouraged to set a communication challenge for yourself.

→ ## How satisfied are you with your communication ability and the outcomes you achieve?

What is your belief about how you communicate? Do you feel that you represent yourself well or do you feel that you keep falling into the same old traps and land up compromising your wishes? If you are feeling stressed or pressured, how does this affect your ability to communicate? Or, if you are facing hostility or a direct challenge, what happens to your capacity to communicate?

Exercise 3

To help you get started on examining your communication style, habits and tendencies, use the tables below to get some simple measures.

On a scale of 1–10 (with 10 being 'all the time' and 1 being 'not at all') rate yourself on:

	1 = Not at all	2	3	4	5	6	7	8	9	10 = All the time
A: How often do you feel **satisfied** with your communication ability?										
B: How often do you get the **outcome** you wish from your communications?										

Have a look to see how these two measures compare. If they do not both occupy a position at the top end of the scale – say between 7–10 – your communication challenge will be immediately apparent. An example of this is shown below:

	1 = Not at all	2	3	4	5	6	7	8	9	10 = All the time
A: How often do you feel **satisfied** with your communication ability?										✓
B: How often do you get the **outcome** you wish from your communications?	✓									

If 'A' is greater than 'B', it suggests that you are doing something that sabotages your intended message. You may feel that you are communicating in a clear and concise way but it seems that people aren't always receiving you in this manner. Do you hold a set of values that denies you a satisfactory outcome? Are you always trying to please others?

Do your responses look like the ones shown on the next table?

	1 = Not at all	2	3	4	5	6	7	8	9	10 = All the time
A: How often do you feel **satisfied** with your communication ability?					✓					
B: How often do you get the **outcome** you wish from your communications?					✓					

If 'A' is equal to 'B', it suggests you know what you're doing and you can predict what you get! It may be that you're effective (both ticks at the high end of the scale) or ineffective (both ticks at the low end of the scale). The example above suggests an 'average' capability; a capability that you may wish to enhance, perhaps.

If both your scores fall into the '9' or '10' category, you could be supremely assertive or, you may have tipped into a more aggressive style. An aggressive approach ensures you get the outcome you wish, and you may well be very satisfied with your ability to communicate your wants, however, its effectiveness is short-lived as people eventually find ways to redress the power balance.

Or are your responses more like this:

	1 = Not at all	2	3	4	5	6	7	8	9	10 = All the time
A: How often do you feel **satisfied** with your communication ability?	✓									
B: How often do you get the **outcome** you wish from your communications?										✓

If 'A' is less than 'B', it suggests that you're more effective than you think but you don't know why! Indeed, you may have a clear intention about what you wish to communicate, and you may manage to convey that intention but equally, you may feel that you don't do it in the most effective, sophisticated or concise way.

Now think about what happens when you're stressed or pressured. Recall three instances when you've been overtaken by a situation or when you've been shocked and caught off guard. What happens to your communication abilities then? Note these on the template below:

Examples of my communication when I'm stressed or caught off guard:	This is how I communicated in those instances:	This is what I notice about my style when I'm rattled:

What happens when you get rattled by something unexpectedly? Do you get snappy? Do you walk away? Do you lose control? Are you inflexible and unable to communicate openly? Or, do you suddenly feel clear in your thinking? Find that you're able to access your thoughts and get really articulate? Gather your wits and communicate with calm precision?

When we're stressed or thrown off guard, we tend to be propelled straight back into our Neanderthal brain which caters for survival. In this state, we'll use any method of communication that comes easily to us.

Now that you've identified your tendencies when under pressure, think about what your ideal set of responses would look like. How would you like to communicate in times of stress? Seed this in your mind for now and use it in some of the later exercises when you're pursuing your communication ideal.

When I'm stressed, my preferred communication style would be:

This was just a quick 'dip stick' measure of the level of satisfaction you have with your communication style and its effectiveness under pressure. It represents the 'thin end of your developmental wedge' and indicates the size of your challenge and the level of commitment you'll need to take yourself forward into assertive waters.

→ Identify your style – what are your communication habits and tendencies?

To refine the diagnosis further, let's have a look at the style of communication you generally adopt. This will explain why you are satisfied or dissatisfied with the way you communicate and point towards the specific steps that you'll need to take to enable you to do so assertively.

Exercise 4

Below you'll find an assertiveness questionnaire. Try to answer the following questions as accurately as possible by selecting a letter 'a', 'b', 'c' or 'd' that most resembles your *general* approach. When you have done so, circle the associated number in the matrix below the questionnaire.

As you are responding to the questionnaire, think carefully about the evidence that you're drawing upon to answer the questions. Are you sure you have the right one?!

1 **When I complain about a product or service:**

a I generally leave with a satisfactory outcome and on good terms with my counterpart.

b I always get what I want!

c I don't complain because I don't feel able to exert my rights.

d I often find myself walking away feeling angry about an unsatisfactory outcome. I think about what I 'should' have said.

2 **When a conflict arises:**

a I tend to avoid conflict because I feel unable to express myself – and I'd probably be responsible for the conflict in the first place!

b I just shrug my shoulders, disengage and walk away without saying anything.

c I go in with a determination to win – and I do!

d I manage to express my point of view without offence.

3 **In a meeting, when I want to make a point:**

a I make my point in the hope that others will agree with me. If they don't, I disengage and refuse to contribute again.

b I express myself boldly and hammer home my point until everyone agrees with me.

c I make my point clearly and listen to others' responses. I may adjust my thinking if my view has been changed.

d I don't make a point because I don't have anything valuable to say!

4 **In a contentious situation, if I am asked my opinion:**

a I tell people that I don't really have an opinion on that matter.

b I share my opinion and ask others what theirs is.

c I always have one and believe it is the 'right' one!

d I will disclose my opinion but I may do so flippantly or sarcastically.

5 **If someone asks me to do something I'd rather not do:**

a I tell them 'No!' and there's no way they're going to dump that on me!

b I say 'I'd rather not' but if they pressure me, I'll begrudgingly say 'OK' and feel really fed up with them.

c I tell them that I am unable to help them on this occasion.

d I tend to agree to others' requests so that I can avoid confrontation.

6 **Sometimes I need to ask for support or assistance from those for whom it is not their responsibility. When doing so:**

a I don't ask people to do things for me.

b I just tell them what I need and pressure them to do it.

c I explain my needs and ask if they are able to help me.

d I deliver the contrary message in the hope that they'll pick up my need. For instance: 'I don't suppose you'd be willing to...?'

7 When I go into a room of strangers:

a I feel confident and assume that they'll want to talk to me.

b I think about who I'm going to introduce myself to and what they'd be interested in talking about.

c I dread meeting new people because I never know what to say to break the ice!

d I avoid meeting new people at all costs!

8 When someone asks for feedback:

a I tell them they were 'fine' but in my head, I tell them how it really is!

b I just say they were great and leave it at that. I can't give feedback.

c I share my perceptions of their behaviour based upon a real situation and offer an alternative way of dealing with it.

d I give it to them between the eyes!

9 When I'm asked to do something that I wasn't expecting:

a I remain clear-headed and choose my response appropriately.

b I seize the opportunity to demonstrate my capability and talents.

c I try to hide but if that doesn't work, I just do as I'm told.

d I'm always the one to get put on the spot. I really hate it and do the least I can get away with.

10 When others get their way instead of me:

a I get mad and resolve to get even.

b I think of ways in which I can sabotage them.

c Others always get their way over me.

d I recognize their rights and get on with what I'm doing.

11 When I find myself in an unusual or tricky situation:

a I am comfortable and feel fully confident.

b I notice that people look to me for guidance and seek my lead.

c I look for someone to tell me what to do.

d I try to find a way out without being noticed.

12 If I am involved in a debate:

a I always win because I'm more than happy to drive my opinion home.

b I don't share my opinion because no-one would want to hear it anyway!

c If someone doesn't listen to my view I disengage and distract myself with something else – doodling, looking out of the window, texting.

d I like to listen to others' arguments and respond with my own. I am curious and focus on the outcome rather than my input.

13 If someone needs my help to further their career:

   a I can't think why they're asking me and I don't see why I should help them get ahead of me.

   b I see it as an opportunity to put them on the wrong track.

   c I like to coach others so I give them my time and attention and help them identify the best way forward for themselves in spite of the consequences to me.

   d I do what I can to help them even if it disadvantages me.

14 If I make a fool of myself:

   a I laugh at myself and move on.

   b I think others have conspired to sabotage me and resolve to get back at them.

   c I'm bound to be the fool!

   d I accuse others of setting me up and get angry.

15 When I'm a member of a new team:

   a I wait until I'm told what to do.

   b I wait until I'm invited to enter the team but the 'best roles' have usually gone by then.

   c I make sure everyone knows I'm the leader.

   d I try to find out what people are good at and what part they'd like to play in the team.

16 When I go to a new country:

a I like to observe the new culture I'm experiencing so that I can be thoughtful about how I interact.

b I get swept along and sometimes enjoy the experience.

c I love to get straight in to the thick of things and make myself known.

d I just know no-one will understand me so I cast a critical eye around before I do anything.

17 When entering change situations:

a I know change can be challenging so I make sure I know as much as possible and communicate my thoughts and feelings.

b It's bound to be dreadful so I hold my breath and co-operate when it suits me and not when it doesn't. It's 'their' job to persuade me that it's going to work!

c I just get carried along and, if I don't make too many objections, I'll probably end up being OK.

d I relish the thought of shaping the outcome of the change.

18 When I look at successful people:

a I think 'It's OK for them. They've had ...... support/resources/luck!'

b I respect their success and appreciate my own equally.

c I think, 'Yes! I'm one of those!'

d I couldn't imagine people thinking that I'd be that successful.

19 If I'm asked my opinion unexpectedly:

a I give it!

b I might say that I'd be willing to share it but I'd like to think a little before I do.

c I think they're trying to catch me out!

d My mind goes blank and I say 'I don't know'.

20 When someone has something they want to say:

a I listen attentively and tell them I'm fascinated by their tale.

b I sigh inwardly because they love the sound of their own voice.

c I'm curious about what they're saying and ask lots of questions.

d I tell them to get on with it because I don't have much time.

21 When I encounter someone with a different set of values or personality to myself:

a I like to explore the differences in our world views.

b I give them a lot of space to express themselves in their own way.

c It is too much effort to adjust to someone else's views and style.

d I think that they're 'wrong' and I'm 'right'!

22 If I'm in a difficult situation:

a My ability to communicate my wishes is undiminished.

b I like to be aware of what's going on so that I can make some sound decisions about what to do.

c I keep my head down so that no-one asks my opinion about what to do.

d I wait to be told how to handle things.

23 People tell me:

a I'm competitive and always seek to win.

b I'm even handed, respectful of others and seek a win/win solution.

c I bow to others' authority resentfully.

d I say 'yes' too easily and get walked all over.

24 I think I:

a Am confident and am prepared to put myself out there.

b Represent myself honestly and give space to others to do the same.

c Am somewhat unable to challenge others openly but do find other ways of making my opinions felt.

d Am rather timid and unassertive. I often feel overlooked.

Your circled scores in the matrix should look something like the example below which illustrates two responses.

The first is where someone has answered 'b' for question 1.

The second is where they've given answer 'd' for question 2.

When you have completed the questionnaire, total each column up so that you have a score each for 'a', 'b', 'c' and 'd' – and then total these up to arrive at a 'grand total'.

Question number	a	b	c	d
1	4	①	3	2
2	3	2	1	④

Use the following matrix to record your responses:

Question number	a	b	c	d
1	4	1	3	2
2	3	2	1	4
3	2	1	4	3
4	3	4	1	2
5	1	2	4	3
6	3	1	4	2
7	1	4	2	3
8	2	3	4	1
9	4	1	3	2
10	1	2	3	4
11	4	1	3	2
12	1	3	2	4

13	2	1	4	3	
14	4	2	3	1	
15	3	2	1	4	
16	4	3	1	2	
17	4	2	3	1	
18	2	4	1	3	
19	1	4	2	3	
20	3	2	4	1	
21	4	3	2	1	
22	2	4	1	3	
23	1	2	4	3	
24	3	1	4	2	*Grand Total:* 'a' + 'b' + 'c' + 'd'
Total					

Check your overall score against the paragraphs below. Does one of these describe you?

If you score between **72–96**, you're probably enjoying an *assertive* style of communication that enables you to manage your world according to your own wishes whilst also honouring others' right to manage their world equally autonomously. However, if you are at the higher end of this scale, ask yourself if there are times when you are 'overly assertive' and likely to trespass on others' rights to assert themselves. If there was a debate about whose rights had precedence, yours or your counterpart's, who would win?

If you score between **48–72**, you probably feel unassertive and unable to take command of your own communications. You may feel victim to circumstance, or susceptible to others' whims and influence. Do you feel frustrated with yourself when you find yourself on this familiar territory over and over again? This is often called a *passive* style of communication. It does not indicate that you are a passive person in essence, just that you don't do yourself, or others, justice in the way you communicate. As a result, you may be perceived to be a bit of a pushover and those that want to delegate responsibility will often do so in your direction, knowing that you're unlikely to make any objection. If you feel put upon in this way, ask yourself what your communication style looks like to observers and whether or not you are 'inviting' this type of imposition.

If you score between **24–48**, your ability to communicate assertively may depend upon your mood or the level of confidence that you have at the time. Or, it may be determined by external factors that are beyond your direct control. For instance, you may find yourself in a situation that calls for an assertive response – such as saying 'No' to a request – but you haven't managed to psych yourself up in preparation for it. If this describes you, it would suggest that your communication abilities are determined by circumstance or chance. In other words, you may happen to come across a situation that favours your assertive abilities just as you may come across situations that steal these capabilities away from you. There may be times when, failing to communicate your message, you display subtle (or not so subtle) signals that you are not happy. This can take the form of a deep sigh, turning your back or rolling your eyes whilst failing to put words to these implicit messages. It may also take the form of a grudge, which results in you looking for opportunities to take revenge for the communication faux pas that you feel was imposed upon you. This type of communication style is called *passive-aggressive*. It generally stems from a sense of powerlessness.

If you have a score between **0–24**, however, it is worth checking that your assertive capabilities have not migrated towards an *aggressive* style. Aggressive communication puts you at the centre of the exchange whilst eliminating the other's right to be heard and to make choices. An aggressive style can certainly be an effective way of getting your needs met. However, this style won't sustain relationships with assertive people, as they'll quickly get fed up and decide whether or not to play your game. Instead, you may find yourself surrounded by those who are less able to assert themselves. Although you may feel that they are dependent upon you for your clarity, confidence and direction, over time, you may find that you are dependent upon them for helping you feel good about yourself. Ask yourself whether your style is overly domineering and, if you really don't know, ask a trusted friend or colleague to give you some feedback.

→ Different ways of thinking about the four communication styles

To help you conceive of your communication style, you may want to think about where you're coming from when you begin a communication – your life position or basic belief about yourself. Of course, this may vary from situation to situation but generally, we colour our communications from a characteristic vantage point in terms of the basic beliefs we hold about ourselves.

Building on the work of Eric Byrne, the founder of Transactional Analysis (TA), Franklin Ernst plotted four life positions on a grid called The OK Corral. Using the term 'OK' to suggest a healthy self-esteem or healthy regard for another and 'not OK' to suggest a lack of self-esteem or poor regard for another, Ernst imagined what it would be like if people with these different life positions encountered each other in their various permutations.

Before you examine the OK Corral, however, take a minute to think about where you're coming from.

Which permutation do you believe most accurately characterizes you?

Life position	✓
I'm OK and You're OK	
I'm OK and You're not OK	
I'm not OK and You're not OK	
I'm not OK and You're OK	

Now have a look at how you would be positioned on Ernst's OK Corral below:

I'm not OK, You're OK	**I'm OK, You're OK**
You're 'better' than me	Mutual regard
I'm not OK, You're not OK	**I'm OK, You're not OK**
I'm no good and you're no good either	I'm better than you

In the box that you have claimed as your own, note the kinds of interactions that are implied by your life position. You can do this by asking yourself:

▶ What kind of communication does my life position tend to attract? (Co-operative, hostile, argumentative, discursive ...)

▶ How do I feel when I enter a communication? (Good, resentful, resigned, satisfied, ready for a fight ...)

▶ What outcome do I generally get? (Win, lose, compromise ...)

▶ What do people say about my ability to communicate? (Skilled, confusing, effective ...)

Now compare your responses with the ones in the OK Corral below. Have you missed something out or does it suggest that you've misdiagnosed yourself?

I'm not OK, You're OK	I'm OK, You're OK
You're 'better' than me: Passive You win/I lose	Mutual regard: Assertive I win/You win
Putting others first Being the 'underdog' I'll put myself out for you Your agenda takes precedence over mine	Collaborative Respectful of different views Curious about other's thoughts Confident in ambiguous situations
I'm not OK, You're not OK	**I'm OK, You're not OK**
I'm no good and you're no good either: Passive-aggressive Lose/Lose	I'm better than you: Aggressive I win/You lose
If I lose I'll find a way of making you lose too I'll get you somehow, but you won't see me do it	Domineering Seeking victory Competitive Winner takes all

→ Setting your learning agenda

How do you feel about the results of the survey you have just taken and the exploration into your life position? Have they revealed a habit or a pattern that you are not happy with? Perhaps they have made you realize that you are better than you thought! Perhaps you have determined that your communication style is a bit 'strong' and needs adjusting to allow space for others. Whatever your response, it is up to you to decide what to do with your results.

On the diagram below, position the result you got from taking the survey and considering your life position. (A shaded example has been included.) This is your starting point. Have a think about how far you'd like to take your development and mark a realistic destination for yourself. This is your goal – at least, for now!

I'm not OK, You're OK	**I'm OK, You're OK**
You're 'better' than me: Passive You win/I lose	Mutual regard: Assertive I win/You win
Putting others first Being the 'underdog' I'll put myself out for you Your agenda takes precedence over mine	Collaborative Respectful of different views Curious about other's thoughts Confident in ambiguous situations
I'm not OK, You're not OK	**I'm OK, You're not OK**
I'm no good and you're no good either: Passive-aggressive Lose/Lose	I'm better than you: Aggressive I win/You lose
If I lose I'll find a way of making you lose too I'll get you somehow, but you won't see me do it	Domineering Seeking victory Competitive Winner takes all

In order to take the right steps and to reap the rewards of your development, it is important, not only to know where you're starting from and what your destination looks like, but to have a battery of practical tools that you can use to help you on your way. In the following chapters, you'll be helped to think about what you can do to reach your communication goal.

Summary

In this chapter, we've taken a diagnostic look at your communication style. You should, therefore, have a pretty good idea about your strengths and areas of development.

If you still are in the dark about how you are perceived, ask a few of your close colleagues, friends or family to give you their honest view of your communication style. Then you can start planning how you're going to enhance its effectiveness.

Where to next?

In the next chapter, we'll focus on what the non-assertive forms of communication look and sound like and why people adopt them. Also, we'll look at what assertive communication styles look and sound like and why these might serve you better.

What have I learnt?

→ What have I learnt about my communication style?

_____

_____

_____

_____

_____

_____

_____

→ What feedback have I got to confirm this perception?

_____

_____

_____

_____

_____

_____

_____

➜ What is the basic belief I hold about myself that determines my communication style?

_____

_____

_____

_____

_____

_____

_____

_____

➜ What skills do I need to develop to ensure I communicate assertively?

_____

_____

_____

_____

_____

_____

_____

_____

Assertiveness meets other forms of communication

In this chapter you will learn:

▶ *what the triggers are for your communication style*
▶ *how you respond to an aggressive person*
▶ *how you respond to a passive person*
▶ *how you respond to a passive-aggressive person*
▶ *what your survival response is*
▶ *the mechanism and power of visualization*
▶ *the nature of a collusive relationship*
▶ *how to give and receive feedback.*

In the last chapter, you were guided through a diagnosis of your preferred communication style. Although you may not adopt this style all the time, you probably default to it when you are not thinking particularly hard about your communication skills.

When you venture into assertiveness for the first time, it quickly becomes obvious that the skills and techniques of assertion are simple and robust. Indeed, they work on a practical basis and provide you with the tools you need to be an effective communicator in many different situations. As you now know, they are based upon consideration for others, as well as oneself, and they are not complicated to learn. However, there is more to assertiveness than this.

When you examine the assertiveness methods, you'll find that they lead you into a deeper understanding of yourself and the values you live by. As a way of becoming more conscious and confident, learning about self-assertion is about as effective as any other self-development approach. This is because being assertive does not take place in a vacuum where everyone else is following the same protocols.

Assertive people have to deal with other communication approaches; approaches that may push old buttons in them. For instance, what do you do as an assertive person when you encounter an aggressive person who reminds you of being bullied at school? Do you find yourself being pinged back to those past times and react as you would have done then? Or, what do you do if you encounter a passive-aggressive person who reminds you of your grandmother where, perhaps, the hidden message is loaded, complex and difficult to field? Encountering these opposing styles can be a forceful reminder of your own patterns, bringing to the surface 'stuff' that you felt was buried years ago.

This chapter will explore the meeting point between two styles and help you work out how to deal with them.

→ Aggression

Many people succumb to those whom they perceive to be stronger than themselves, thereby giving up their power. This is, of course, exactly what the aggressive person is aiming to achieve.

What are the characteristic behaviours of an aggressive person?

▶ They are often loud – but not always.

▶ They seem to be overly confident.

▶ They get exercised easily and project lots of energy.

▶ They may go red when they get excitable.

- ▶ They look for others' weaknesses.
- ▶ They dominate and expect to get their own way.
- ▶ They are ego driven and want to win at all costs.

What other aggressive behaviours come to your mind?

▶ _____

_____

_____

▶ _____

_____

_____

▶ _____

_____

_____

▶ _____

_____

_____

▶ _____

_____

_____

It is tempting to think that those who live by aggression are necessarily extraverts and those who live by passivity or passive-aggression are introverts. This is not true.

All personality types are susceptible to all styles of communication. So, when you are making your observations, remember that aggression is NOT correlated with being an extravert and passivity or passive-aggression is NOT correlated with being an introvert. Different communication styles are behavioural and NOT determined by personality.

Let's look at how you deal with aggression.

When you think about people who use aggressive behaviours, what feelings emerge in you? Tick the box that most accurately describes your feelings.

Your response to aggression	✓
Fury – How dare they treat me like this!	
Self-preservation – I must get out of here!	
Paralysis – I'm stuck. I don't know what to do!	
Surrender – I'll be safe if I co-operate	

You may recognize these different responses, respectively, as:

▶ 'fight'

▶ 'flight'

▶ 'freeze'

▶ 'roll over' and 'yield'.

These are natural responses to danger, or a perceived threat. They have enabled the human species to survive for millennia so they are thoroughly tried and tested and have become hard-wired into our systems.

However, the level of threat in the modern world is not equivalent to that which was encountered at the dawning of man. At this time, because animals were predatory and humans were competing for resources, these responses were a matter of life or death. Today, however, it is rare that you are fighting for your life so, when these responses are triggered, they no longer serve us as they did. Yet all the adrenalin that prepares our bodies to fight, take flight, freeze or yield, has to go somewhere, or be repressed, and repressed energy has a knack of leaking. It either goes inward, where its leakage can be felt as passivity or passive-aggression, or it leaks out, where it is expressed as aggression.

So, unless you are naturally assertive and able to discern 'what's yours' and 'what's not', or able to distance yourself from the aggressive triggers when you encounter them, you are likely to find yourself adopting one of the other styles of communication. Which one is favoured by you? Do you go into passivity? Passive aggression? Or do you try to meet aggression with aggression and enter the battle for victory? (This last option is the most risky for when 'win-lose' is being pursued by both people, there will be no prisoners!)

Exercise 5

Think about the threatening situations that trigger your 'fight', 'flight', 'freeze' and 'roll over' responses (remembering that 'threat' in our current context is likely to be a threat to our ego, agenda, values or some other intangible threat). You might want to look at your professional and personal styles to see if they're different.

Which situations trigger your 'fight', 'flight', 'freeze' and 'roll over' responses?

	Describe the kind of threatening situation that gives rise to your 'fight', 'flight', 'freeze' or 'roll over' response
Fight	e.g. When someone offers me solutions before properly appreciating the problem!
Flight	
Freeze	
Roll over	

Describe what you do when you experience one of these responses?

	Describe the behaviours you typically adopt when you are in the grip of 'fight', 'flight', 'freeze' or 'roll over'
Fight	e.g. I get quite insulting and start picking holes in the other's argument or behaviour
Flight	
Freeze	
Roll over	

If there is a pattern in your responses to the above two questions, it would seem that you're adopting the same communication style regardless of the situation you are in. If, for instance, you always take a 'roll over' approach, you're probably considered to be somewhat passive.

This would make it hard for you to encounter someone who is more aggressive than you.

If the approach you choose is driven by the circumstance, you may be cleverly assertive and choosing the most effective style for the best outcome or you may be flailing around erratically because you don't have a communication strategy. Being pushed and pulled by circumstance (although arguably demonstrating your ability to be flexible) is not 'assertive' as you are not in control of your communication, rather it is the external environment, over which you have no control, that determines your style of response.

Let's consider what drivers are possible in an aggressive person:

▶ They may have had to develop aggressive strategies to survive (at school, in the family, at work ...).

▶ They may feel inadequate in their abilities and skills to deal with situations.

▶ They may feel threatened/frightened.

▶ They may be trying to prove something.

▶ They may be being bullied (as well as being a bully).

▶ They may be naturally aggressive.

▶ They may not understand the situation fully and are boxing with shadows.

▶ They may know more about the urgency of a situation than you do.

Can you think of others?

▶ _____

▶ _____

▶ _____

When you examine this list, there is not one item on it that is strong – even if the aggressor's behaviour can be experienced as 'strong'. And, there is not one item on the list that is about you – even if the aggressor's behaviour can be experienced as personal. Aggression, therefore, does not denote strength nor is it personal. Perhaps these possibilities begin to give you clues about how you might respond to aggression.

Let's think about that and develop some assertive strategies for dealing with an aggressive person.

Try to:

▶ Identify what is being triggered in you: 'fight', 'flight', 'freeze' or 'roll over'. This will allow you to kick-start your pre-planned communication strategy.

▶ Put yourself safely to one side (metaphorically speaking). It is not about you. From this safe vantage point, try to empathize with the other and ask yourself, 'What is driving this?' You could try making this explicit by saying something like 'I can see you're really upset about this. Will you help me understand what's going on for you?' Make sure you keep eye contact so that the aggressor knows that you're not going to be cowed but that you're prepared to listen. Being able to be curious (in spite of the heat and dust!) enables you to ask questions that will throw light on the 'real' situation. 'I'd like to understand more about ..., would you explain the situation to me?'

▶ Reflect back your understanding to ensure you have received the correct message. You could say something like: 'May I just check with you that I've understood the situation correctly?'

▶ Give them feedback on the impact that their behaviour is having on you and ask for a different style of engagement. You could say something like: 'When you shout like that I feel really threatened and uncomfortable. I'd like to come back to this discussion another time when we've had a chance to think about things more clearly.'

Try not to:

▶ 'Go parental' on the aggressor. Phrases like: 'Control yourself!', 'Pull yourself together!' or 'I'm not going to speak to you until you have calmed down!' merely puts you in the heart of the battle for control.

▶ Use comments like: 'Look here!', 'Let me make it crystal clear!' They feel patronizing and are likely to raise the temperature, not lower it!

▶ Interpret their motivations: 'You've obviously got an agenda here!'

▶ Criticize them personally: 'You're just being foolish!' Nothing like a personal insult to fan the flames of fury!

▶ Highlight the points of divergence/disagreement

We know, from neuroscientific research, that to rehearse something in our head fires exactly the same synapses in exactly the same sequence as if we were doing it in reality. And, we know that the more we do something, the more habitual and natural it becomes. Together, these phenomena describe the power of visualization. So, imagine yourself tackling aggression in the way that you choose, applying the techniques that suit your values and style, and rehearse the language you'd like to use so that it becomes familiar to you. Then, when you adopt it in a real situation, it will flow easily and feel authentic. (Creative visualization will be addressed in greater detail in Chapter 10.)

Now, let's look at how to tackle a passive person.

→ Passivity

The passive style of communication is submissive. It conveys the message 'I'm not OK!' and invites dominance and control. The power that is given away by the passive person is usually picked up by others and used to enhance their own. The passive person may also imagine that a superior power to theirs exists in their world. Through this belief, they concern themselves with what they are 'allowed' to do and what they are not. This orchestrates their behaviour and they project the message 'I'm not OK!' but 'You're OK!' This lopsided dynamic sets up an 'I lose' scenario and it can become a bit of a game whereby, whenever the passive person perceives themselves to have 'lost', they say: 'I told you so. I always lose!' Yet, the behaviours that they adopt conspire to create and perpetuate the 'I lose' dynamic and they hook themselves into it as if they were destined to live it out forever.

Who do you know who projects a passive demeanour? What do you notice?

▶ low energy

▶ a willingness to take the blame

▶ an inability to say 'No!'

▶ they tend to minimize their physical impact

▶ they can easily become anxious and uncertain and seek validation

▶ they tend not to put themselves forward

▶ they may disengage from what's going on.

What other passive behaviours come to your mind?

▶ _____

_____

_____

▶ _____

_____

_____

▶ _____

_____

_____

▶ _____

_____

_____

_____

▶ _____

_____

_____

When you conjure up an image of a passive person, what feelings do you have?

Your response to passivity	✓
Irritation, impatience and then you ignore them	
A tendency to get directive with them and tell them what to do	
A temptation to get drawn in and solve their problems for them	
An attempt to motivate and energize them	
Is there another response that you have?	

Although passive people tend to make themselves as quiet and as invisible as possible, their strategy is, strangely, quite powerful because it calls to 'the rescuer' in many people. They depend, therefore, on others noticing their passivity and responding to it with the intention of assisting or resolving a problem for them. For this reason, passive behaviour *can* be quite overt and noticeable. It may even be spoken out in self-deprecating messages such as: 'I'm hopeless at ...', 'I haven't a clue about ...', 'I can't cope with ...', 'I need someone to help with ...' Indeed, through this overt abdication of self-responsibility, a passive person is able draw others to them where, together, they enter a pattern of victim-rescuer. This is where the 'victim' seeks help and the 'rescuer' seeks control. It is called a 'collusive' relationship as both parties are supporting each other's hidden agenda.

Sometimes a passive person is unwell or clinically depressed and has withdrawn from the world because they don't feel able to cope with it – and they really don't want to be rescued. This is when it becomes a pathological condition and there's little you can do about it other than suggest they seek professional help.

Notwithstanding this, let's develop some assertive strategies for dealing with a passive person.

Try to:

▶ Remember that their style is their choice and don't let it draw you in.

▶ Deal with and react to what you are presented with.

▶ Encourage them to take responsibility for entering the communication – you can do this by asking open questions such as: 'What do you think?', 'How do you feel about this?'

▶ Give feedback on what you are experiencing so that they can't avoid knowing the effect that they're having. You could say something like: 'When you don't communicate, it makes me feel that you're not interested. Would you give me your thoughts please?'

▶ Be empathic inasmuch as something may be going on for them that results in uncharacteristic passivity.

Try not to:

▶ Get irritated and resort to aggressive behaviour.

▶ Rescue them.

▶ Muscle in and take over.

▶ Over-compensate for their lack of engagement by placing an undue amount of attention on them.

▶ Exaggerate your energy in the hope that they will pick up some of it.

▶ Attempt to persuade them, through rational argument, to participate more fully.

Passive people are generally not *trying* to be difficult. They're probably fighting internal messages of doubt that disempower them and prevent them from meeting people on equal footing. It's certainly worth giving them a chance to show themselves in a more positive light but if it doesn't work, don't feel that you have to make it work on their behalf. They will not change their behaviour if everyone always tries to make things OK. There comes a time when you have to walk away and let them experience the full consequences of the responses they have evoked. In this way, they can decide for themselves whether or not they wish to perpetuate this style of communication.

Now let's look at how to tackle a passive-aggressive person.

→ Passive-aggression

The passive-aggressive form of communication is hidden, covert and tends to be sabotaging. It conveys the message 'I'm not OK and you're not OK either!' It is quite similar to the passive communication style in the sense that it manifests as a withdrawal from a person or an event. However, it is more actively focused on generating negativity, such as 'getting revenge', whilst denying any scurrilous agenda and appearing to be supportive. (Perhaps even adopting a crocodile smile!)

Passive-aggression is, therefore, a hidden form of aggression. Usually, the person feels pretty powerless so the only way they can cope with this is to 'steal' power from others without them being fully aware of what's going on. Mostly, they have to enjoy their satisfaction in private because to come out into the open and be transparent about their motivations and deeds would compel them to take responsibility for their poor behaviour, and that's not what they want to do. They like the protection of the hidden world.

Who do you know who projects a passive-aggressive demeanour? What do you notice?

- ▶ They appear to be 'hard done by' or 'aggrieved' (they may moan or grumble about things).

- ▶ They may sigh and roll their eyes whilst agreeing to do something.

- ▶ When challenged, they are likely to deny there's a problem.

- ▶ They may avoid your eye totally or gaze at you insolently. Their eye contact doesn't 'feel' genuine.

- ▶ They may be polite – but through gritted teeth.

- ▶ They may avoid issues rather than tackle them.

- ▶ They may pout, sulk and feel sorry for themselves.

- ▶ They may find ways of sabotaging you such as missing deadlines or being late for meetings.

What other passive-aggressive behaviours come to your mind?

- ▶ _____

_____

_____

- ▶ _____

_____

_____

- ▶ _____

_____

_____

▶ _____
_____
_____
_____

▶ _____
_____
_____

When you conjure up an image of a passive-aggressive person, what feelings do you have?

Your response to passive-aggression	✓
Self-doubt because you hold negative thoughts about someone else	
Frustration because you have a suspicion that something is going on under the surface	
Concern that you're going to be sabotaged, but you don't know where and when	
Unaffected because you pay no attention to this behaviour when you see it	
Is there another response that you have?	

Unlike passive behaviour, which we have already identified as overt, passive-aggressive behaviour is covert. When in the presence of this style of communication, we can usually sense that something is wrong, but the power of a passive-aggressive person is dependent upon them keeping things below the surface so they try to avoid any explicit 'leakage'. This gives us two choices. Firstly, we can try to ignore the behaviour in the hope that it will go away. Secondly, we can risk embarrassing ourselves by confronting it and finding that we are wrong. Both of these options discourage us from doing anything about it so the passive-aggressive person 'wins' by ensuring everyone 'loses'!

However, we know that this behaviour can only exist in the shadows of denial, from both parties. (The passive-aggressive person is in denial of their true feelings and the other party is in denial that it is occurring.) So, this points towards a strategy for dealing with it.

Let's develop some assertive strategies for dealing with a passive-aggressive person.

Try to:

▶ Remain focused and true to your own agenda.

▶ Keep calm and remember that this is about them, not about you.

▶ Be empathic and recognize that this is an uncomfortable place for them. This style of communication has probably arisen from some unpleasant experiences in their lives.

▶ Expose their agenda by giving them feedback on their behaviour. You could say something like: 'It appears that you're unhappy with this discussion. Would you tell us what's going on for you?' Whether they make a public denial that they're unhappy or admit to what's going on for them, they have had to take responsibility for their position, which is something that a passive-aggressive person is trying to avoid doing.

Try not to:

▶ Give a disproportionate amount of attention to the passive-aggressive person.

▶ Accuse them of being unco-operative, disruptive, sabotaging.

▶ Meet passive-aggression with passive-aggression.

▶ Assume you know what game they're playing and accuse them of something specific. Like trying to get your job!

Practised passive-aggressive people are skilled at making you feel as if you're the fool. The game is intricate and complex and not easy to deal with. If you don't manage to surface the motivation of the passive-aggressive person, ensure you are alert to any evidence that your theory about their motivation is correct. It may be that you need to protect your back by ensuring that others have your story from your own mouth before a distorted version reaches them from a passive-aggressive mouth. Ignoring unpalatable behaviours is no protection from someone who has perfected these sabotaging skills.

We've looked at the less seemly side of aggression, passivity and passive-aggression yet sometimes, the energy that characterizes each of them can be used positively.

When used with a positive mindset, when can these communications styles be helpful?

Aggressive	Passive	Passive-aggressive
Useful when you need to protect yourself or others	Useful when you are surrounded by hostility	Recognizing passive-aggression in yourself demonstrates self-awareness and perhaps motivates you to develop a different style?
Useful in an emergency when you need to direct people	Useful when you need to survive	Passive-aggression in yourself enables you to recognize it in others?
Useful to help you stick at your personal goals	Useful when you need help from an expert, such as with a doctor or surgeon	Actually, it's hard to find occasions when this is helpful!
Useful to help you overcome obstacles		

You'll probably have noticed that one of the tools that appears frequently in this workbook is giving, and getting, feedback. Giving feedback is not an easy technique and many people are fearful of using this method as it may be received as criticism.

Here's a quick tip for *giving* feedback. It is called the **AID** model.

> **A** = Action (this is the behaviour that I've noticed and this is when I noticed it).
> **I** = Impact (this is the impact that your behaviour had on me).
> **D** = Different outcome (this is what you could have done that would have led to a different outcome).

As with all assertive tools, use your own data when giving feedback. Never give feedback on hearsay. And use the first person to demonstrate that you're taking responsibility for what you say. Never use 'referential power' by referring to what someone else thinks who happens to be more powerful than both of you.

If you're *receiving* feedback in this form, you have an opportunity to understand how the other person's perception was formed because they saw your behaviour directly. When the feedback has been delivered, just say 'thank you'.

Summary

This chapter has surveyed how the different modes of communication encounter each other and what you can do to get the best from conflicted communications.

Giving and receiving feedback has emerged as a central tool in the armoury of assertive techniques. Although it is 'delicate' territory, it is worth perfecting this skill to re-direct communications and to make them more open and authentic.

Where to next?

In the next chapter, we'll be deepening your awareness of your style and building on the notion of getting feedback.

What have I learnt?

→ Typically, what situations do I encounter that trigger my 'fight', 'flight', 'freeze' or 'roll over' response? (Who or what presses my 'crumple button'?)

_____

_____

_____

_____

_____

_____

_____

→ What reactions do I get when I 'fight'?

_____

_____

_____

_____

_____

_____

_____

→What do people say when they've seen me take 'flight'?

_____

_____

_____

_____

_____

_____

_____

→What do people say when I 'freeze'?

_____

_____

_____

_____

_____

_____

_____

4 Getting to the root of the problem

In this chapter you will learn:
- ▶ *how (trusted) others see you*
- ▶ *how to observe yourself and reflect on your communication style*
- ▶ *how to get feedback from others*
- ▶ *how you make your choices*

The exploration so far has been about the different forms of communication that exist: assertive, aggressive, passive and passive-aggressive. Hopefully, this will have laid the foundation for you to strike off in a new direction and make more sense of your preferred style, and the styles you resort to when you are unsure or unprepared for a communication.

Exercise 6

When you think you have yourself taped, so to speak, and you are pretty sure you have captured your communication style accurately, write down on a piece of paper what style you think you adopt most frequently and add a note of those that you tend to slip into in different circumstances – like when encountering someone in authority, someone who is bullying, someone who seems weak, someone who you feel is manipulative or someone you *really really* like.

Fold your paper in half and put it to one side.

→ Now, go to a colleague or friend that you trust and ask them the following question:

1 'If you were to choose overall, what do you think my communications style is?' Give them the four options – and try not to argue with them about their opinion. Instead, ask them some clarifying questions such as...

2 Can you give me an example of when you've seen me demonstrate that style?

3 Have you noticed any other types of communication that I have used in your presence and if so, what are they and when did I adopt them?

4 If I were to make some changes, what changes do you think would benefit me most?

→ Thank you!

Now, offer them your piece of paper and ask them to compare their answers with yours. Is there a difference? Have a conversation with them about any differences that have emerged from this exercise. They are likely to be able to throw light on these differences and give you examples of where their perceptions have come from.

Mark these differences on the form below. It will help you stand back and be more objective about your communication style(s).

You could repeat this exercise using people from different compartments in your life. For instance, is there a difference between the way you are perceived at work and in your personal life?

They see me as: / I see myself as:	Assertive	Aggressive	Passive	Passive-aggressive
Assertive	*			
Aggressive				
Passive				
Passive-aggressive				

There is an obvious point of victory on the grid which is marked by the star! All the other spaces on the grid offer you a challenge in terms of your communication development agenda.

If there is a difference between the way you see yourself and the way others see you, you will have learned something new about yourself – or confirmed a suspicion that your true style has shown itself. Whatever the reason for this discrepancy, the fact that it exists suggests that there's some work to be done. When there is misalignment between your communication strategy and the way your communication is received, you have a problem. You may protest that 'they're not getting it' and that your motivations should be 'obvious' to them but they might not be 'getting it' because you have misjudged the means by which you transmit 'it'! And, their perception is what you have to deal with, particularly if it doesn't align with your reality.

A point to ponder:

It is the responsibility of the communicator to ensure that their message has been received accurately. It is not the responsibility of the recipient to try to work it out.

So, what would it take for you to close the gap between yours and others' views of your communication ability? And, how will you know that you have gained an accurate understanding of how others perceive you?

Self-awareness is at the root of assertiveness and it goes hand in hand with exercising choice about how you communicate. So, how do you develop a high level of self-awareness, and how do you make your choices?

Let's look at self-awareness first. How do you deepen this if you don't know what you don't know? Here are some ideas:

→ Self-observation and reflection

Try filling in the matrix below.

This is what I believe I do well (Self-observation)	This is how I see myself doing it (Reflection)
e.g. I give entertaining presentations	I use the reactions from the audience to connect with my experience and build funny stories.

'Sit on your own shoulder' and observe yourself in communication with others. This may sound a little strange but one of the qualities of being human is the ability to step back, take a distanced view of ourselves and contemplate our opinions, behaviours and beliefs in an objective way. It's a bit like watching ourselves on film and either liking or disliking what we see. We talk about 'This is what I believe'. But how do you know what you believe? It implies that there's a believer, and an observer (or knower) wrapped up inside you. You can use this duality to gain new information about yourself – but beware of your own self-fulfilling fantasy. It might be worth checking out that your observations are shared by others to ensure that they see you the same way that you do. If they don't, they may give you some feedback, which is another way of learning about yourself!

→ Getting feedback from others

The following section will help you get the feedback you need, and includes a series of grids for you to complete.

This is what I believe I'm doing well	This is how others see me doing it
e.g. I use the reactions from the audience to connect with my experience and build funny stories.	I've learned that sometimes I embarrass the audience rather than entertain them. This is down to my language.

For instance, if you think you're good at giving entertaining presentations (as in the example above) and you seek feedback to verify this, you may find that others see your skills differently. They may say something like, 'I like the confidence with which you give presentations and it is true that the audience laughs out loud. And I think you could curb your language more because sometimes the laughter is embarrassment!' If you receive a piece of feedback like this, ask the person who is giving it to you to give you specific examples of what they've seen so that you can recall the moment and relate to it. For instance, you might ask them about the situation in which they observed you and what language you used that they thought led to embarrassment.

You might not agree with them but at least you'll be alert to it next time you give a presentation, and you may find that there's a grain of truth in it. Seeking feedback adds another layer of objective observation to your own and, if you ask a few others, you may find a pattern emerging. To build your picture further, ask yourself if you've received this feedback in other contexts.

Feedback from others

This is how others see me	This is the pattern I've noticed
e.g.	
Feedback 1: My language can embarrass	I don't seem to read people very well and can be seen to be unempathic.
Feedback 2: Sometimes I make fun of people	I've had this feedback in my personal life too!
Feedback 3: I say things that others would probably not say	
Feedback 4: I can get very personal and make people feel uncomfortable	

This is how others see me	This is the pattern I've noticed

Noticing the patterns in your life – I always seem to make people feel awkward! – offers you an opportunity to change your approach. You will see from the worked example how consistent messages build into an informative pattern, especially when they're given to you in different contexts. This can set an agenda for your own development – if you want it to.

NOTICING THE RESULTS YOU GET

This is what I'm trying to do	These are the results I'm getting
e.g. I'm trying to be more aware of the impact of my communication and I've started asking people for	Someone thanked me for my diplomacy the other day! I'm being told that I'm much more considerate to those with whom I'm communicating and they like what I'm trying to do.

CELEBRATING YOUR SUCCESSES AND TRIUMPHS

These are the things I do really well – and others agree with me!

→ How do you make your choices?

Consider for a moment how you actually make choices. Do you:

▶ Think logically about them, analysing all the permutations and consequences.

▶ Act intuitively, based on gut feeling?

▶ Use your values: what's 'right', what's 'wrong'?

▶ Apply theories and frameworks to your choice?

▶ Find a similar situation, comparing it to the one you're facing, and apply some of your observations?

▶ Draw from your experience?

▶ Take advice from others who have more experience than you?

▶ Observe a role-model – 'What would Gandhi do?'

Exercise 7

See if you can place yourself on the following scale. Does your placement differ from circumstance to circumstance or do you always make choices in the same way?

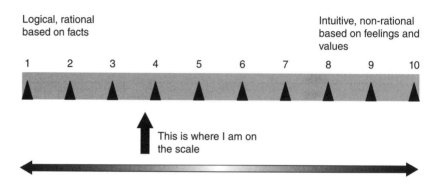

If you have placed yourself between 1 and 4, you are likely to use facts and figures to support your choices. Although these concrete measures are credible from a scientific perspective, when they're used to support your arguments, they can feel quite cold and unyielding. Think about how those who are on the other end of the scale may feel as they observe you making your choices and encounter your decisions – and consider how they might feel when you use facts and figures to support your arguments. They may experience you as quite aggressive when you dismiss their objections with certainty based upon a logical analysis. Also, think about those times when facts and figures are not relevant in choice-making, such as when you're comforting someone who is distressed or attempting to motivate a member of your team who feels disenfranchised. How do you proceed then?

If you have placed yourself between 7 and 10, you are likely to use your gut feeling to inform your choices. Although you may feel that your choices are 'obvious', they may not seem dependable to those who prefer a more structured approach. Watch you don't assume others have the same values and style as you do. They may feel vulnerable taking instruction from you when you can't verify your decisions with scientific rigour.

....

The way you make choices has nothing to do with how assertive you are, but knowing your style does enable you to articulate your choice credibly and accommodate the needs of those coming from a different perspective. It will also enable you to explore each other's rationales openly to gain understanding and reach an agreement.

Exercise 8

Thinking about your own preference, are you 100 per cent intuitive? Or perhaps 40 per cent logical, 60 per cent intuitive? If you're not sure, what do people say of your approach to making decisions and solving problems? Mark your position on the diagram below: All 'head'? All 'heart'? Or a mixture of both?

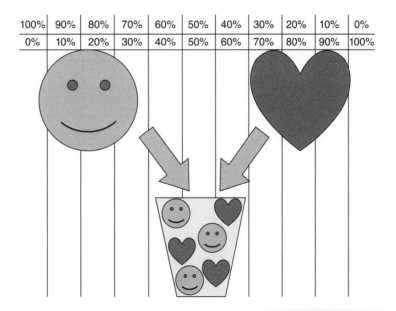

What would it take to redress the balance so that you could complement your decision preference with its opposite counterpart?

Here are some ideas:

► Rehearse your argument with someone who has a different preference and get them to ask you questions about your rationale.
► Develop the habit of asking yourself how you 'feel' about your choice.
► Develop the habit of asking yourself how you could explain the logic of your choice.
► Look at the problem and ask yourself: 'Is it a *feeling* problem or is it a *thinking* problem?'
► Try writing it down to see if you can make a persuasive argument.
► Try speaking it out to see if you can make a persuasive argument.
► Ask for feedback from an objective third party.

See if you can find some other options:

► _____
_____
_____

► _____
_____
_____

► _____
_____
_____

Once you are able to articulate your rationale, you'll be able to make your point assertively.

Summary

This chapter focused on deepening your self-awareness through reflecting on your preferences and getting feedback from others. The reason for doing this is that self-awareness is the root of self-assertion. If you don't understand yourself well, or the impact you have on others, it is very difficult to be convincing when making a point or forming persuasive arguments.

Where to next?

In the next chapter, the focus will be on how you can choose your communication style. You will gain tips and tools to adopt in different circumstances.

What have I learnt?

→ What is the most illuminating piece of feedback I've received lately?

_____

_____

_____

_____

_____

_____

_____

→ What causes the behaviour that I've been given feedback on?

_____

_____

_____

_____

_____

_____

_____

→ When I make choices how do I balance my head and my heart and what is the effect of this on others?

_____

_____

_____

_____

_____

_____

_____

→ What am I curious about in myself and, therefore, what self-observation will I focus on?

_____

_____

_____

_____

_____

_____

_____

5 Choosing an assertive communication style

In this chapter you will learn:

▶ how to focus on what's happening 'in the present moment' and slow down time
▶ how time and space may determine your communication style
▶ the 'paybacks' and 'penalties' of the different communication styles.

Having identified your natural communication style, this chapter is going to focus on how you can adopt an assertive strategy in different situations.

Often, people who aren't naturally assertive, find that they get spring-boarded into situations where they resort to their 'old' communication style. Usually, this is because they haven't had time to prepare and rehearse what they want to say so their old habit kicks in. Then, afterwards, they beat themselves up and say: 'I should have said this!' or 'I wish I'd said that!' or 'Why didn't I say the other!' ... and then they feel despair!

Wouldn't it be great if you could slow down time sufficiently for you to choose your best response and deliver it with authority? Well, you can, to an extent; just like when you fall and it feels like it's happening in slow motion – but it's not! However, in the space that is created by that 'time is slowing down' feeling, you think about how to land, what would happen if you hurt your wrist, who's going to pick you up, how embarrassed you're going to be and what you can do to minimize the damage to yourself or the thing that you're carrying.

Which situations trigger your 'old' communication style?

In which of these situations do you resort to your 'old' communication style?	✓
When an unexpected situation arises that demands an immediate response – such as someone pushing ahead of you in a queue	
When you want something that isn't catered for in the service you're using	
When you're under pressure or stressed	
When something really matters to you	
When you are going to an authority figure 'cap in hand'	
When someone disagrees with you	
When someone is frustrated or angry with you	
When you've made a mistake for which you feel guilty or sorry	
When you're in a hurry	
When you're visiting your mother and/or father who gave birth to your communication style in the first place!	

Exercise 9

You've probably fallen, slowly or – heaven forfend – had a car crash slowly. Tick in the grid below the things that you noticed when you were falling/crashing. There is space at the bottom to add your own. **I was aware of:**	✓
The trajectory of my body/car	
What I was carrying/observing	
What I was wearing	
How I should land	
The noise I was making/not making	
What I'd be prevented from doing because of injury	
My breathing/my stopped breathing	
The expression on my face	
Who was watching	
What the person watching would think	
How I looked	
Being embarrassed	

What do you notice about the items on this list? Is there a golden thread that pulls your responses together and what is it?

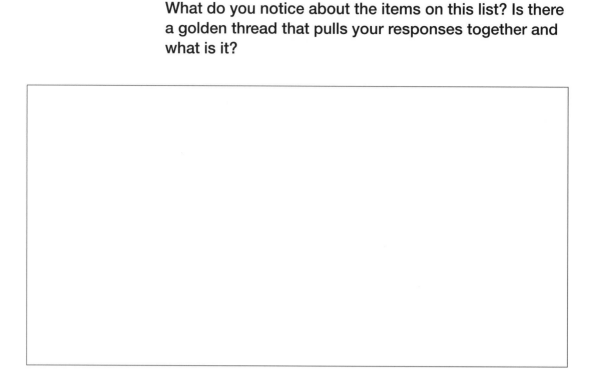

It's interesting, in just a few seconds, how much you can focus upon and how able you are to build a complete picture of what's happening at the time.

By reversing this logic, would it be true to say that being focused enables you to notice many details and slow down time?

You might also notice that you didn't have time to become frightened whilst you were falling. You entered the experience unexpectedly and therefore, didn't have time to tap into your anxieties or fears. When you become frightened, you tend to contract (in preparation for 'fight', 'flight', 'freeze' or 'roll over'). When you manage your fear, you are open to receive more information that enables you to deal with what is happening now and what matters now.

By following this logic, would it be true to say that if you manage your fear, you'll be better equipped to see the complete picture and slow down time?

These two points may seem somewhat oblique, but they are designed to help you think about how you can create the time and space to operate in full awareness and autonomy, despite time pressures that may otherwise push you into your habitual patterns.

Have a look at the matrix below and see if you can identify the different situations that put you in the different boxes. (The time continuum goes from 'little' to 'lots' as it travels from left to right. The space continuum goes from 'low' to 'high' as it travels from the bottom to the top. 'Space' can be seen as the amount of exposure or visibility you experience.)

Little Time, Lots of Space	Lots of Time, Lots of Space
Too little time and lots of space can lead to a feeling of exposure and vulnerability. It can prevent you from accessing the thoughts and skills you need to be in charge of your communication. This is when you might say: 'I wish I'd said something else!'	Ample time and space enables you to make conscious choices and establish new habits. Being calm and focused creates a feeling of time and space in which to choose. This is when you might say: 'I said what I meant and meant what I said!'
Unexpected exposure	**Choosing your communication style**
Too little time and space results in pressure and the reassertion of old habits of communication. This is when you might say: 'I always fall into the same trap!'	Lots of time but little space may encourage you to work things out in your head but may also prevent you from practising your communication strategies and getting feedback. You may develop assertiveness in theory, but not in practice. This is when you might say: 'I know what to do but I never get to do it!'
Old habits die hard	**Theory, not practice**
Little Time, Little Space	Lots of Time, Little Space

Try answering these questions:

By considering the matrix above:	
Is there a box that you tend to occupy more than others?	
Can you recall and describe an occasion when you were in this particular box?	
What was going on for you at that time? (Work-related challenge? Social situation? Professional or personal pressures? Celebrations? Were you coerced or did you volunteer? Who witnessed you? What was the outcome?)	
What would have to change for you to occupy your preferred box?	
Does this suggest something you could do differently?	
What will you try to do differently another time?	
When will you put this idea into action?	

So, choosing to be assertive is helped when you create the time and space to make the choice consciously. This means sufficient time and space to allow you to interpret the 'real' message that you are receiving. Thereafter, to decide how you feel about it, how you'd like to respond to it, how to access the tools and techniques that you need to respond in the way you choose and finally, it allows you to send your message assertively.

Exercise 10

Here is a time and space creating exercise for you to try:

Next time you're in a room full of strangers, rather than find ways of retreating so that you don't have to introduce yourself to anyone or feel like a wallflower, stand still and create time and space in which to summon your assertiveness capabilities.

Try this:

▶ Stand stock still as long as you can. (Create strong body posture. Stand up straight, feet planted side by side but a short distance apart and look out into the room directly.)

▶ Be fully present, breathe deeply and bring your attention to the event. (Try to silence the voices that tell you that this is your worst nightmare, that you're rubbish at meeting new people, that no-one will want to talk to you and that you always make a fool of yourself.)

▶ Instead, take time observing the layout of the room. See where the food and drink is located or the display of brochures. Create an internal map so that you feel comfortable in the environment.

▶ Amble over to the refreshments and find something that you'll enjoy.

▶ Look around the room to see who's talking to whom. Is there anyone you know who you could approach? If not, have you identified someone that you'd be interested in talking to?

▶ Move towards someone intentionally and introduce yourself. You could use a number of different opening lines: 'You seem to be having an interesting conversation, may I join?' 'I've never been here before but I'm looking for 'x', do you know what he/she looks like?' It doesn't really matter what you say, the fact that you're hearing your voice in the void is more important. It helps you break your own ice, so to speak.

► Prepare a 'point of view' so that you have something relevant to say that says something about you. (This should be relevant to the purpose of the event.) You wouldn't just 'land' in a conversation with this point of view but if you have something to work towards, it will give your conversation purpose and direction and fill the gap that might otherwise open up after you've introduced yourself.

► Pick up a thread and work with it – or break away with a polite comment and start again.

It doesn't matter whether you're an introvert or an extravert. Remember, being assertive is not correlated with your personality. Your communication preferences are behavioural and you've learned them over your lifetime because they reward you in one way or another and, the more they are rewarded, the more established they become as part of your behavioural arsenal. Here are some of them – and not all are entirely functional or positive!

Aggressors are rewarded because people do as they say. They feel dominant and powerful and people will turn to them readily when they feel weak and need to adopt someone else's strength.

On the other hand, these same people may curse the aggressors' behaviour behind their backs and lose the will to remain loyal after a relatively short time.

Passives are rewarded because they can opt out of taking responsibility for themselves and they tend to be rescued by someone who feels pity for them. They may become the object of someone's 'cause' and be cosseted and cared for, sometimes for a lifetime.

One the other hand, passives may never embrace the fullness of their potential or take control of their lives. They may miss out on extraordinary opportunities that would enrich and fulfill them because they give themselves over to someone else.

Passive-aggressive types are rewarded because people tend to collude with them. They are appeased frequently (which feels pretty powerful to them) and often remain unchallenged as to their 'true' agenda, which is almost inevitably sabotaging in some way.

On the other hand, passive-aggressive people may not enjoy fulsome relationships. If their agenda is always hidden, and if they are not properly disclosing, people will tend to mistrust them and discredit anything they say. This strategy may fail in the long term, therefore.

Perhaps some of these passages help you to see yourself in a new light. You may not embody the full extent of any of these categories, but you may identify strategies that you use which take something from the behavioural descriptions above. If you are wondering whether any of your strategies have been observed by others, ask for feedback from someone who is on your side and who is prepared to work with you to bring you into a more assertive communication style.

Summary

This chapter has explored how you create time and space in which to choose your communication style.

Once you are practised at the art of slowing things down so that you can make the intervention you choose, you will find that it seeds a new habit in you that you can return to when you need it.

As you go through this workbook, you will find other ways of building on this notion. Learning to say 'No!' or 'Yes!' is one additional skill that will help you create the context for being assertive as will the subject of body language and the use of gestures, both of which will appear in subsequent chapters.

Where to next?

In the next chapter, you will be invited to think about how your preference for accessing information and thinking about it affects your communication style.

What have I learnt?

→ How am I going to slow things down to create the time and space in which to manage my communication choices?

_____

_____

_____

_____

_____

_____

→ How will I keep my attention focused on the present and not on the past or the future?

_____

_____

_____

_____

_____

_____

➜ When do I feel conspicuous and less able to manage my communications and when do I feel safe and able to choose my responses?

_____

_____

_____

_____

_____

_____

_____

➜ What rewards or paybacks do I seek from my preferred communication style?

_____

_____

_____

_____

_____

_____

_____

6 Living – and choosing – in the present

In this chapter you will learn:
▶ whether you live in the 'real' or imagined world
▶ how the focus of your mind can affect your decision-making capabilities
▶ how to use your preference for 'imagination' or 'facts and figures' to deepen your understanding of your communication approach
▶ to put yourself in others' shoes and understand how they perceive you
▶ to take as much responsibility for how your message is received as you do for how it is transmitted.

We live in a world where drama and sensation rule the media. As a result of this perpetual backdrop to our lives, we are attracted to situations that arouse fright or delight in us. By tapping into the drama of a situation, we can ensure that there's always something going on that's remarkable; something to share with our friends and acquaintances. Mostly, this pursuit is pretty harmless; indeed, it can be really entertaining. However, it can also remove us from being fully present and dealing with life as it presents itself to us. When we take our cue from a dramatic experience and run with it, we enter the heady world of its effect. This can feel as real to us as if it were actually happening. However, it's not *really* happening, it's only happening in our minds – and in our bodies. Our emotions may rise, our indignity may be ignited, our hearts may palpitate and our breathing may speed up. We can experience reactions as if we were actually in our fantasy, living it out and taking it to the next level. However, any decision that we make or any action that we take at this time can be based on a false premise; a premise conceived in our imagination.

Some of us have particular personality types that predispose us to 'living in our heads'. This can be a blessing and a curse. A blessing because it enables us to access the world of make-believe, of new ideas, of poetry and prose. If you have this preference, you may have heard those in your close circle say: 'Come back to earth. You've gone off on one again!' Or, you may hear them say to a newcomer to your circle: 'She lives in her head you know!' They may say this with a degree of amusement and affection but there's a message there; 'your feet don't touch the ground'! If this is you, ask yourself how much control you have over the musings of your mind. Can you indulge your imagination when you choose or does it dominate your life? Does it remove you from reality where your attention is required? Does it help you deal with the world assertively?

Exercise 11

To determine to what extent you 'live in your head', try answering the following questions:

1 Do you create scenarios in your head that explain others' motivations and behaviours?

2 Do you like to gossip?

3 Can you get mad just by thinking about something that happened in the past?

4 Have you been told that you have a rich imagination?

5 Are you always coming up with new ideas/ innovations?

6 Are you considered a bit of a daydreamer?

7 Do you like to debate philosophical issues?

8 Do you make decisions on imagined 'facts'?

9 Do you tend to worry about things over which you have no control?

10 Do you love a conspiracy theory or a scandal?

11 Do you think in leaps and bounds (linking ideas and thoughts that others find hard to follow)?

12 Do you have a 'sixth sense'?

If you have answered yes to more than half of these questions, it is likely that you distract yourself from what's going by inventing stories. When something doesn't turn out as you imagined, you may hear yourself saying: 'But I thought.......x, y and z!'; an extrapolation that may have taken you miles away from what is actually going on.

....

Beside the obvious 'up side' to this tendency, ask yourself whether you can bring yourself back to the concrete world when you need to. When you encounter something important or serious, will this inclination get in the way of you being able to respond appropriately?

Imagine queuing at a traffic light and the person next to you is signalling for you to hold back by raising their hand. You may think, 'how dare they try to stop me from pulling away from the red light rapidly. They're just trying to push in!' So, you ignore their gestures and, when the light changes, you attempt to roar away and leave them in the dust – only to find that you've driven onto broken glass, have a flat tyre and find it difficult to control your car.

If, instead, you'd asked yourself why someone would be gesticulating to you at a traffic light and wound the window down to enquire, you may have saved yourself embarrassment and, possibly, an accident!

It is hard to be believably assertive when you are boxing with images and shadows!

By contrast, there are others who pride themselves on 'living in the real world'. Instead of following their trains of thought into the more fanciful realm, they rely upon facts, figures and the evidence they see in front of their eyes. Although the more imaginative types may think that these people miss out on opportunities and possibilities, those with a preference for the tangible feel that they live life fully, but with their feet on the ground.

Exercise 12

To determine to what extent you 'live in the real world', try answering the following questions:

1 Do you require evidence before you believe anything?

2 Do you seek facts and figures to back up your decisions?

3 Do you dismiss anything that is born of others' imagination?

4 Are you intolerant of gossips and people who worry?

5 Do you research your decisions and plan carefully how you'll put them into practice?

6 Do you seek inspiration from others who have succeeded in doing what you want to do?

7 Do you rely upon your experience when resolving a problem or issue?

8 Do you pride yourself on your practicality and realism?

9 Do you take what people say at face value?

10 Do you tend to believe that if you can't touch it, feel it, measure it, then it's not worth considering?

11 Are you told you have 'common sense'?

12 Do you like to live in the 'here' and 'now'?

If you have answered 'yes' to more than half of these questions, it is likely that you use facts and figures to make your decisions and dismiss anything that you can't verify as 'factual'. As with the person who tends to live in their imagination, there are blessings and curses with the more factual preference.

....

Think about a situation where you are renovating your home and you seek three quotes for the work you want to do. You notice that there is quite a variance between each quote so you go for the cheapest because it is closest to your budget.

Once the building work begins, you find that the builder is absent a great deal and leaves the site in a mess. You make enquiries and find that he has sent out many low-end quotes and is juggling several projects at one time.

Because you didn't imagine why the quote was low, you left yourself vulnerable.

It is hard to be believably assertive when you see only facts and are ignoring others' motivations!

Of course, both of the examples above are 'extreme' and you'll probably say that you incline yourself to one or the other rather than fully embody it. However, see which of the scenarios is more familiar to you and ask yourself whether you are sabotaging yourself when seeking to be assertive.

Exercise 13

One way of diagnosing your preference is to create a collage or drawing of your life.

▶ Get a large piece of paper and lots of paints, crayons, magazine images, glue, glitter and bits and pieces that you feel depict your life.

▶ Your task is to depict your life from the beginning to the current point using the art materials as your medium.

▶ Enjoy positioning the significant events, places, people and interests that you have. Add your education and work life, the formative 'highs' and 'lows' that you've experienced and anything else that you feel reflects your life story.

▶ Go to town and embellish your work until you're completely satisfied with it. Choose from the full palette of your art materials.

Stand back and have a look – preferably with a trusted friend who can ask you questions about the positioning, colouring and content of your picture.

- ▶ What do you notice?
- ▶ How is your life story depicted? In a straight line or are the events depicted randomly?
- ▶ Where did you start on the paper? Did you start at the left hand side and move towards the right hand side or did you start with an image of yourself in the middle and all the events emanating from you like petals on a flower?
- ▶ How did you create your image? Did you use paints, crayons or pictures cut from a magazine? Did you use sequins, sparkles, bright or sombre colours? Did you use only one colour?
- ▶ Were you literal or metaphorical as you conveyed your life story?
- ▶ Are there events in your life that you feel have created your communication foundation stone – or taken your communication foundation stone away?

Your picture will say something about your approach to life and what you carry into it from your formative years. Don't try to over-analyse your efforts. This is not therapy. Rather, it is an interesting look at how you reflect your significant life experiences – using metaphors and your imagination or using facts and realities.

Do you tend to:

- ▶ Use your imagination to gather information about the world?
- ▶ Use facts and figures to gather information about the world?

If it is the former, remember that others don't have access to your imagination so they may not always understand what you're talking about. To them, it may appear that you're making leaps of abstraction which are hard to follow and therefore don't make sense. This does not help you in your quest to be assertive.

If it is the latter, remember that you may come across as pedantic or dogmatic. By relying on tangible information, you may be less able to capture the attention of others and bring them alongside. This does not help you in your quest to be assertive either.

....

Being assertive requires you to place as much attention on the person receiving your message as it does on the way you send your message. By building a 'bridge' to them, you'll be able to meet somewhere in the middle. This will enable you to raise the chances of a meaningful connection.

When you understand your tendencies, you can create strategies to protect yourself from falling into the same trap over and over again. You can:

▶ Imagine what you'll feel like when you're in control of your communication. Conjure up a rich picture so that you'll know what you're aiming for and recognize it when you reach your ideal.

▶ Ask for guidance from someone with the opposite tendencies.

▶ Reflect on the times that you felt less successful in being assertive to see why. Once you understand this, practise a different approach so that you can find a different way forward.

▶ Observe someone who you admire being assertive to see what tactics they use. If it feels authentic, try them out for yourself.

▶ Rehearse a different set of responses to situations you encounter frequently – either in your mind or out loud. Then, when you need them, they'll be ready for you to use.

Summary

This chapter focused on how to create time and space in which to access your assertiveness skills and then looked at your imaginative or analytical preferences that might affect your ability to be assertive. By letting go of the 'stories' in your head or by putting 'facts' into the wider context of others' motivations, you may be able to tap a more assertive style of communication.

Some ideas about how to change your communication pattern have been offered. See if you can find some more of your own.

Where to next?

The next chapter will explore how you can say 'No!' or 'Yes!', both of which can be notorious traps for non-assertive people.

What have I learnt?

➔ How do I like to gather information on which to base my choices? Hard facts or feelings and intuitions?

_____

_____

_____

_____

_____

_____

_____

➔ How do I react to those who have the opposite preference for gathering information?

_____

_____

_____

_____

_____

_____

_____

→ When does my preference work well for me and when does it have unhelpful consequences?

_____

_____

_____

_____

_____

_____

_____

→ What assumptions do you make about people who have different preferences to your own?

_____

_____

_____

_____

_____

_____

_____

7 Saying 'No!' – and saying 'Yes!'

In this chapter you will learn:
▶ *about your susceptibility to saying 'Yes!' when you mean 'No!'*
▶ *why you can't say 'No!'*
▶ *what values you hold most highly*
▶ *when your values kick in and empower your 'No!' response*
▶ *when your values factor against your ability to say 'No!'*
▶ *some techniques for saying 'No!'*

We're beginning to make progress in our exploration of assertiveness.

Already, a number of topics have been examined, including the lure of stories that take us away from realistic and relevant conversations which require us to say what we mean and mean what we say. By feeding on the 'empty' drama that our minds can conjure up, we can get distracted from what we need to do to get us on track and in the driving seat of our lives.

When you notice that you've moved inside your head and that you're building a story, just tell yourself to 'Stop it!' Managing this tendency is a matter of applying your will and preventing yourself from indulging in the fanciful ups and downs of your chosen drama.

The next challenge facing you is that of saying 'No!' – or 'Yes!'

Have a think about the situations in which you find it difficult to say 'No!'

Here are some likely candidates:

▶ A colleague approaches you with a smile and a request for help. It's really not your job but you cannot find it in you to say 'No!' You end up adding their task to your 'to do' list.

▶ A family member needs a favour. They flatter you into yielding to their request. After all, you're SO dependable!

▶ Your boss explains that there's a crisis looming and that you're the perfect person to help. You end up spending half your weekend doing work that sits outside your role description.

▶ A friend asks you to cover for them while they escape their responsibilities. You don't feel happy about this but you agree to their request.

▶ A neighbour asks you to receive a parcel that they're expecting to be delivered that morning. You agree to this and stay in until mid-day but it still hasn't arrived.

▶ You're planning an indulgent evening in with a glass of wine, a take-away and a film. Your sister asks you to babysit at the last minute because she's been let down by her regular babysitter.

In all these situations, you've been handed responsibilities that belong to someone else. You may feel that there are good reasons for you to take the onus for these tasks, and you may decide to say 'yes', but beyond this:

▶ What capability do you have to choose whether you want to assist or not?

▶ How able are you to say 'No!' just because you want to?

► On what basis do you feel able to say 'No!'? (Do you feel that you need a reason or an excuse to justify your response?)

If you're looking for the justification to say 'No!' it indicates that you don't feel that you have the 'right' to choose for yourself. Indeed, you'll probably be looking for a legitimate reason, a rule, or an excuse, that you can fall back on that others will feel is justifiable. It's that grey area which is so hard to be firm about and it's to that grey area that, unerringly, people go when they want something from you. It's almost as if they know you are weak there and that if they press you hard enough, you'll concur with their wishes – and they're probably right because you've probably concurred with them before and they see it as a bit of a pattern of yours.

It doesn't take many instances of you taking someone else's load for them to have an expectation that you're an 'easy touch'; and this expectation will be fuelled with the confidence of experience. This makes it even harder to say 'No!'

When you try to argue yourself into saying 'No!' you may think: 'I can't say "No!" because my friend won't care for me any more.' Or 'It's my boss's request and I don't want to appear disloyal or unco-operative.' Or 'Family is important. I can't create difficulties because I'm stuck with them for life!' Whatever argument you use, you lose. You lose because you diminish your right to choose. Indeed, you probably imagine the consequences of saying 'No!' (in full 3D technicolor!), thereby weakening any resolve you may have to make your own choices.

Exercise 14

Fill in the following table, to try and work out what you fear when you say 'No!' to someone's request.

What do you fear when you say 'No!' to someone's request?	✓
They won't like/love me any more	
I'll be considered selfish and unsupportive	
No-one will help me when I need help	
I'll be passed over for promotion	
I'm flattered that they think I can help!	
It makes me feel useful/important/liked	
They'll blame me for not helping if things go wrong	
I'm skilled and efficient so it won't take me as long as it would take them.	
They'll take out their frustrations or anger on me as soon as they get a chance	
I won't be included any more	

If you examine all these responses – and you may have some more of your own – you'll probably notice that you're putting yourself in a secondary position to others. You're giving your power away and allowing others to dominate you. When you do this, you're sending the message that you're not in control of your own life and that you depend upon others for your sense of well-being. People learn very quickly that you're not robust in your ability to say 'No!' and they'll continue to make requests of you for as long as you let them.

It's no good expecting others to take responsibility and do your choosing for you. If you find yourself protesting that their request is 'not fair' this is a signal that you're not taking command of your own world. People will seek and find what they want to fulfill their needs. There's no incentive for them to consider your situation and refrain from making a request because they see that it is 'unreasonable'. They will rely on you for a straight answer. They may not like it, but that's not your concern. The consequence of you saying 'No' is their business, not yours!

Exercise 15

Have a think about the situations in which you find yourself susceptible to saying 'Yes' when you want to say 'No!'

Situations where I say 'Yes' when I want to say 'No!'

Equally, have a think about the situations where you are able to say 'No!'

> *Situations where I am successful in saying 'No!'*

Now compare your two responses:

What is the difference between these two situations?	
What's going on when you are able to say 'No!'?	

Everyone has their limits, and these limits are determined by our 'values'. If you think about the requests that have been made of you in the past, you're bound to find that there were some which were non-negotiable. Indeed, there will have been times when 'No!' was inevitable and easy for you to say. If you think about these times, you'll find out what these limits, or values, are for you. By being clear about your values, you'll be able to leverage your resolve and extend your ability to say 'No!'

Your values are the product of your beliefs. They are usually acquired through your family and cultural influences and are in place by the time you reach young adulthood. They form an ethical/moral framework, or meaning-making mechanism, that enables you to determine what's 'right' and what's 'wrong'. You generally enjoy people who share your values because it validates you and enables you to have agreeable, reinforcing conversations. Conversely, you may be repelled by people who hold different values to yours. These contrary values may be picked up in their actions and behaviours or they may be spoken about explicitly.

In summary, values are:

▶ an important and often hidden element in your choices and decisions

▶ an ethical/moral framework that helps you make sense of your life

▶ likely to cause consternation or hurt if someone's values conflict with yours

▶ the means by which meaning is made and the route to the 'highs' and 'lows' of life.

Sometimes values are very strongly held and only emerge when compromised or thwarted – which can be surprising to all concerned!

Have a think about your values. Can you name them? How do they shape your life? If, for instance, you believe that everyone has a right to be educated, one of your values will be 'education' and you may hold the opinion that education should be made available to you, your children and society in general, whatever their level of privilege.

If this value is coupled with the belief that people should help each other, your 'serve others' value may lead you to being an educator through helping others to learn. This may be in a number of different settings, which, again, will be determined by your values. Perhaps you'll collect a TEFL qualification (Teaching English as a Foreign Language) and travel abroad to help people develop their English language ability. Or you may prefer to wield your skills in a private school, where access to facilities and resources are less restricted. Or, perhaps you'll become an academic, undertake research and teach in a university setting.

Your value of 'education' along with your value of 'service' will act as a touchstone for your life purpose, dictate your priorities, inform your decisions and shape your life. Indeed, if your values are being met, it is likely that you will feel that you are being 'true to yourself' and satisfied with your life.

If you have a value around 'work' and a value around 'family', you may find that too much work causes you a conflict of values because it prevents you from satisfying your family value. Also, if you are 'out of work' and have responsibility for a family, you're likely to experience this as extremely stressful. This stress will probably provide the momentum for you to find work, any work, so that you can support your family.

However, if you have a value around 'serving others', this may be where you trip up when someone asks you to do something for them. Have a look at the list below to see if any of these values resonate with you. (This list is a distillation of some of the more prominent values.)

Exercise 16

Consider the values on the following list. Distribute the numbers 1–10 between them. (1 = most important and 10 = least important.) This 'forced choice' will ensure that you consider the values you hold and create a hierarchy of those that are most important to you.

Allocate a score of 1–10 to those values you hold (1 = most important, 10 = least important). There will be some that remain unallocated and therefore less important to you. Don't allow any tied scores. Make sure you come out with a 'top ten' ranking.			
Autonomy/Independence		Determination/Discipline/Hard work	
Diversity/Variety		Education/Knowledge/Personal growth	
Education/Personal Growth		Equality/Fairness	
Freedom/Liberty		Integrity – Reliability/Respect/Honour	
Justice		Peace	
Perfection		Power/Authority	
Prosperity/Wealth		Responsibility	
Rules/Regulations/Law		Safety/Security	
Self-worth/Self-belief		Service/serving others/Generosity/Loyalty	
Stimulation/Excitement		Success/Accomplishment	

When you've identified those values that you hold most strongly, ask yourself if any of them are responsible for disabling your ability to say 'No!' and in what circumstances they are triggered.

What value could you promote in your hierarchy that would enable your 'No!' resolve to kick in?

For example, if one of your scores looked like this:

Self-worth/self-belief	8	Service/serving others/Generosity/Loyalty	2

... it is telling you that you value 'Serving others' more than you value your 'Self-worth'. The priority that you give to other people may well be the very issue that is undermining your ability to choose because, inevitably, you'd choose in someone else's favour. Could you elevate your 'Self-worth' value and diminish your 'Serving others' value so that the balance would weigh in your favour instead? You could always reverse it again in special circumstances.

....

Next time someone asks you to do something that you'd rather not do, remember that you're just as important as they are and tap into your 'Self-worth' value to give you the strength to say 'No!'

Here are some tips that might help you summon your resolve.

To build your strength beforehand:

▶ Stand in front of a mirror and practise saying 'No!' Get used to the sound of your voice so that it doesn't seem strange to you.

▶ Ask a trusted friend to do a role-play with you. Again, you'll hear yourself using the words and you'll develop a language that you can draw upon later.

▶ Review your values and see if you can promote one of your secondary ones into a superior position. For instance, you could promote your 'self worth' value over your 'serve others' value.

▶ Create scenarios in your mind's eye and rehearse them. Make sure you rehearse them successfully and try not to imagine that familiar old feeling of letting yourself down again!

▶ Think of a typical scenario where you're likely to cave in to someone's request and find a phrase that you can use comfortably.

If you're face to face:

▶ Look the person making the request in the eye – and say nothing until they have finished speaking. (If they are leaning over your desk – and if it's possible – stand up so that you are on the same level as them. Whatever, try to keep as still as possible while you hold their gaze. It's much stronger than fidgeting anxiously as your eyes dart back and forth.)

▶ As they're mouthing their request, try holding up your hand in a 'halt' gesture and say: 'I'm going to have to interrupt you there because I'm unable to help you on this occasion.'

▶ Leave a short silence after they have spoken. There's no need to jump in whilst you're considering your response.

▶ Think of a delaying tactic if you need one. 'I'd like to think about that before I commit myself.' Or 'I need to review my diary before responding.'

▶ Just say: 'No. I can't help you this time.' (No apology. No excuses. No reason. If you give a reason, they'll only try to argue it away!)

If you're on the telephone:

▶ Stand up and walk about to command energy and strength. (If it helps to make gestures, do so. They can't see you but they can certainly pick up your resolve.)

▶ Explain what's happening at your end and, if it's inconvenient to talk, ask them to call back later.

Keep a note of your successes and use them to encourage more of the same.

Summary

This chapter has focused on the difficulty of saying 'No!' In the course of doing so, the role that values play in disabling people's ability to decline a request is explored. If saying 'No!' goes against a principle you hold strongly, there is less likelihood of you being able to say it. Indeed, your values can corner you and compel you to acquiesce to requests that you really don't want to accept. However, by raising the importance of your 'self-worth', you'll be able to honour yourself in preference to someone else and make your decision freely. (You may still decide to say 'Yes', but you'll do so because you want to, not because you feel you have to.)

Where to next?

The next chapter is going to focus on your body language. Your body gives away much about you, even if you try to disguise its messages. By being in command of what your body is saying, you can ensure that your verbal and body language are congruent and convey conviction and authenticity.

What have I learnt?

➡ In which situations am I most susceptible to saying 'Yes', when I would rather say 'No!'?

_____

_____

_____

_____

_____

_____

_____

➡ What are the non-negotiable values I hold that enable me to be assertive?

_____

_____

_____

_____

_____

_____

_____

→ Which values, or assumptions, do I notice in those who ask others for what they need or want?

_____

_____

_____

_____

_____

_____

→ How can I use my understanding of others to manage my 'Yes'/'No!' response more assertively?

_____

_____

_____

_____

_____

_____

⑧ *Let your body do the talking!*

In this chapter you will learn:
- ▶ *why body language is so important to master*
- ▶ *what universal messages are conveyed by our bodies*
- ▶ *what makes up a first impression – and how fast it occurs*
- ▶ *how to create a positive first impression*
- ▶ *the importance of your eyes in communication*
- ▶ *what gives the game away – 'leakage'!*
- ▶ *the importance of congruence between the body and the word*
- ▶ *to develop 'presence'*

In the last chapter, you mastered the ability to say 'No!' – or 'Yes', if you preferred. By digging into the reasons for your powerlessness over someone else's request, you could eliminate this disabling loop from your process and come out with a clear decision about whether or not you wanted to assist someone in their endeavours.

Now, we're going to look at how you can enhance your message, or sabotage yourself, with your body.

Body language has received a lot of attention over the last few decades. It seems we are still rooted in our prehistory, when our bodies were the primary means of communication. Even today, the truth of our messages is revealed through our bodies. Our physical positioning, posture and gestures (along with the tone, pitch and quality of our voice) form the elements of a hidden language that gives away what we really think and feel. The study of body language became voguish, primarily, to decipher human courtship rituals, thereby underlining our enduring affiliation to the jungle – and to sex!

Some researchers tell us that more than 90 per cent of what we say is conveyed by our body, rendering this physical, or non-verbal, channel of communication the most powerful. (Of that 90 per cent, around 40 per cent of the message is conveyed by the eyes.) The remaining 10 per cent is the verbal channel; the spoken word. Although there are some who feel these proportions are somewhat exaggerated, it is undeniably true that our bodies 'speak' and that because this 'language' is largely unconscious, our bodies cannot 'lie'.

What's more, body language is pretty consistent throughout the human species. Apart from some notable exceptions – nodding to denote agreement and shaking the head to denote disagreement can have contrary meanings in certain cultures – we are able to interpret the emotions of those who do not share our linguistic heritage with a high degree of accuracy.

The universally shared language comprises recognizable signals of:

▶ anger

▶ boredom

▶ disgust

▶ embarrassment

▶ fear

▶ happiness

▶ pride

▶ relief

▶ sadness

▶ shock

▶ surprise

These emotions are hard to control as they often creep up on us unexpectedly. However, there are ways of bringing your body under control in a way that allows you to reinforce your messages and enhance your assertiveness capabilities. Think of negotiators or poker players, both of whom master the art of looking inscrutable and hiding what's *really* going on for them. (Although, technically, this is aggression in the sense that it's a win/lose dynamic.)

Let's start with first impressions as these often set the tone for future communications and relationships.

It is said that it takes less than ten seconds to create a first impression – and it is disproportionately difficult to shift it once it has been formed. Again, casting back to the days of the jungle, it was important to size someone up rapidly as they may be an enemy. This skill, then, was a matter of survival. It informed our next move – 'fight', 'flight', 'freeze' or 'roll over'. Today, the consequences are not so severe but we still have a tendency to stereotype or bracket people so that we can choose the appropriate response. These shortcuts are useful, as they save time, but they may deny us a deeper connection with those who are less skilled at showing themselves in a good light from the outset.

Assuming that most people do not suspend their judgements, preferring to make snap judgements and compartmentalize someone rapidly, your next job could hang on the first impression you create. Your credibility as a public speaker or presenter could equally be affected by the way you first command attention and your success at building your social network is also facilitated by your creating an immediate connection.

Let's look at what goes in to creating a first impression with someone.

THE 'NON-VERBALS'

▶ the handshake and they way they look at you

▶ the way they walk and their posture

▶ the way they dress

▶ their gestures

▶ the way they smell and their level of attractiveness

▶ their facial expressions – smiling, serious, inscrutable

▶ their general demeanour – relaxed, stressed, anxious, fearful

▶ their level of confidence

▶ their timeliness.

THE 'VERBALS'

▶ the way they greet you

▶ the way they talk – the tone, pitch and rhythm of their speech

▶ the way they listen to you and respond to what you're saying

▶ the questions they ask you

▶ the 'appropriateness' of their remarks.

This is quite a list, and it all happens in a few seconds!

Exercise 17

Now let's appraise your ability to bring all these variables together in one 'killer' moment. Imagine that you're going for a job and you'll be meeting one or two decision-makers who are going to interview you.

Circle a number on the scale to indicate where you are between the two extremes. When doing this, don't get distracted by those rare occasions when you have done something differently. Think about your general approach; the one that characterizes you in your close circle of friends and peers.

Your handshake:

| I take a firm hold and shake their hand vigorously | 1 | 2 | 3 | 4 | 5 | 6 | 7 | 8 | 9 | 10 | I offer the tips of my fingers for a gentle handshake |

Your posture:

| I walk in decisively and stand tall and strong | 1 | 2 | 3 | 4 | 5 | 6 | 7 | 8 | 9 | 10 | I walk in gingerly to avoid looking arrogant and wait for my greeting |

Your greeting:

| I speak first to break the silence. I speak boldly and clearly and look them in the eye whilst shaking their hand firmly | 1 | 2 | 3 | 4 | 5 | 6 | 7 | 8 | 9 | 10 | I wait until I have been greeted and follow their lead. I like to take my time and work out what I want to say |

Your clothing

| I think about what they may be wearing and choose something compatible | 1 | 2 | 3 | 4 | 5 | 6 | 7 | 8 | 9 | 10 | I like to express myself through my clothing so I differentiate myself from them to project my personality |

Your facial expressions:

| I try to smile, convey warmth and be open to forming new relationships | 1 | 2 | 3 | 4 | 5 | 6 | 7 | 8 | 9 | 10 | I tend to be facially serious and restrained, preferring to take my cue from others |

Your general demeanour:

I am very relaxed when meeting new people. I give them all I've got and if they don't warm to me, I don't worry	1	2	3	4	5	6	7	8	9	10	I dislike meeting new people and creating first impressions. I tend to get anxious and inhibited

Your level of confidence:

I am a very confident person. I like being put in challenging situations and pitting my wits against the unknown and unexpected	1	2	3	4	5	6	7	8	9	10	I have little confidence and I try to overcome this by making myself meet new people and try new things. I get exhausted by being in unfamiliar situations

Step back and have a look at the balance of your responses.

Do they tend towards either end or are they clustered in the middle?

Do they vary from one end of the scale to the other as you place your response between the two poles of each question?

Look at your pattern and have a think about the following points:

▶ Clusters indicate a trend or a habit. This might colour the way people see you when they first meet you. Are you happy with this or would you like to change your first impact?

▶ If you tend to place yourself in the middle of the range you could ask yourself if you're coming across as indistinctive. Perhaps you averaged your responses whilst recalling your many different experiences of creating a first impact. Have a think about what types of body language you tend towards rather than what happens every time.

▶ If you had difficulty placing yourself between the two extremes, perhaps you are circumstantially dependent; different occasions bringing out different qualities in you. Perhaps you respond to more formal or professional situations differently from the more social occasion.

▶ Variable responses might come across as inconsistent. You might have a 'limp' handshake, conveying weakness, yet be 'strong' in your body posture. Think about what message this conveys and whether it might be confusing to recipients. Perhaps this is your intention?!

Although you weren't asked the full gamut of questions that go towards building a first impression, the main determinants were there. However, can you think of some more of your own? Do you have a tendency or habit that is visible from the outset? If you don't know, ask someone who has observed you making a first impression. Perhaps you act a little 'sheepish', or even aloof, until you gain your confidence. Perhaps you overdo your 'greeting skills' to compensate for feeling unfamiliar with someone. Perhaps you twist one leg around the other like barley sugar in your attempt to make yourself small.

Ask yourself: If you were meeting yourself for the first time, what would you think? Would you go away with a positive impression?

→ How does your body betray what's going on for you on the inside?

We may think that our thoughts and feelings are private but they 'leak' out in ways that we are not aware of, not only facially but in our 'tics' and in the inconsistencies between our body language and our spoken language.

Most particularly, our eyes are very important in conveying messages without being accompanied by the spoken word. Think of those glances across a room that 'say it all', or those flashes of irritation that betray someone's real feelings in spite of their protestations to the contrary.

WHAT DO OUR EYES SAY?

► I love you.

► I am closed to you.

► I am hiding from you.

► I'm (not) listening to you.

► I'm (not) interested in you.

► I want to understand you.

► I want to 'see' you.

► I am protecting myself from you.

When you're listening to someone, you're probably going to focus on their eyes for most of the time. The speaker's eyes tend to wander, accessing their thoughts and seeking inspiration. It is possible to overdo the gaze. Meter your piercing gaze and be aware of when the other is closing down to you. They may feel that you're intruding on their personal space.

Our physiology also triggers body signals over which we have limited control. Things like your teeth chattering, your shoulders hunching, and your body shivering when you're cold.

WHAT DOES YOUR LEAKAGE LOOK LIKE?

Physically, you may have some habits like:

▶ Folding your arms across your chest when you feel defensive or angry?

▶ Juddering your leg like a pneumatic drill under the table whilst looking 'cool' on the surface?

▶ Nodding or shaking your head in an exaggerated way?

▶ Letting your eyes wander away from the person who is talking to you or focusing on a spot somewhere over their shoulder?

▶ Wringing your hands or biting at the skin around your fingernails?

▶ Advancing into the personal space of others and clutching at their arm? (We all have an exclusion zone around us, which varies from circumstance to circumstance and from culture to culture. It is often referred to as our 'energy field' or 'aura' and we can generally feel when someone has entered it without invitation.)

▶ Twirling and twisting your body in embarrassment indicating that you'd rather be anywhere than where you are?!

Verbally, you may have some habits like:

▶ Finishing off people's sentences for them.

▶ Predicting what they're going to say and interjecting the word that you think they'll choose.

► Sounding a battery of 'uh ha's and 'hmmmm's to encourage them to deliver their message speedily.

► Interrupting and stealing the conversation.

These verbal tendencies will be covered more extensively in the following chapter on 'listening assertively'.

GESTURES

The way we accentuate our messages with gestures adds depth, meaning and drama to what we're saying. However, they must be appropriate, timely and unambiguous.

If we're saying 'Look over there!', we must point in the direction we're wanting someone to look, make the gesture strongly (from the shoulder) and ensure that it is synchronized with the words 'Over there!'

Other timely gestures may include:

► thumbs up

► a wink

► a shrug

► a pointy finger

► punch the air

► a grimace

CONGRUENCE

It is important to stay wise to the traps set by in-congruence. Look at body language as the non-verbal channel of communication and ensure that it is expressed coherently and in tandem with the verbal channel.

An authentic person will demonstrate congruence between the spoken and unspoken word. There will be no counter indications to the messages they send. They won't say: 'You can trust me' whilst shaking their head.

CREATING PRESENCE

It is generally considered that tall people are advantaged. They are assumed to have natural assertiveness and power and, in men, research suggests that they tend to find success more easily than their shorter counterparts – positional, financial and relational.

Yet, the business world has examples of those who do not hold a height advantage, but who do hold a power advantage. Bill Gates and Jack Welch are two of the better known leaders of diminutive stature that have taken their companies to the height of success. How have they done this? Perhaps it is true that shorter men have to resort to more potent methods to equalize the odds for their success?

Is the same true for women? Studies have shown that shorter women are more likely to get married and have children than taller women, who are considered to be the more intelligent, successful and pushy ones.

What is it that enables shorter men to buck the trend and overcome people's natural suspicion about their lack of power, potency and potential? And what is it that enables taller women to dodge the usual epithets when they succeed at business?

Perhaps the answer is the same for both – presence. Whether you're considered too short as a man or too tall as a woman, being able to overcome others' prejudices is a skill to master. The ability to 'appear' bigger or more confident than you are by expanding your energetic impact is one way to achieve this.

Exercise 18

Try this exercise next time you're in a queue:

Engage with your mind and envisage yourself filling the space around you. Move your focal length to the furthest point on the visible horizon and imagine a chord joining you to it from where you stand. Push your power down this chord. You could think of it as electricity passing between you and the furthest reaches of your attention. Think of it illuminating everything that sits between you and your focal point.

Notice what happens around you.

Now do the opposite. Bring the chord back into your body so that it no longer stretches out as far as you can see. Close your energy circuits down by withdrawing your attention from your surroundings and the people in them.

Compare this to your more energized state.

What do you conclude?

You may have noticed that when you extended your focal length and energized the space between you and it, people turned to look at you. They saw that you had presence. Alternatively, when you 'shut down', they walked straight past you without turning their heads. They didn't see 'presence' in your energy. (This exercise does not depend on unusually good looks by the way!)

If it doesn't work at first, try again.

Also, notice those people who do have 'presence' and ask yourself where their attention is and what is happening to their energy.

→ Building closeness and rapport

We use our bodies to reinforce our messages as we build our relationships. Often this is subconscious but we can see it at play if we observe what's going on around us.

Have a look at couples sharing a drink at a bar. As they engage in intimate conversation, their body positions will reflect each other's, creating a form of symmetry, and the level of their drinks will diminish at the same rate. In this way, they fall in step quite naturally and it feels comfortable and intimate. As soon as a contentious issue emerges, they'll 'break' that symmetry and strike different poses that indicate a mismatch in their communications. In general, as far as the body is concerned, a disagreement looks like a misalignment.

Other signals of rapport suggest the quality of symmetry too:

▶ People tend to use similar language when they are engaged in 'good' conversation.

▶ People tend to share the same values when they 'like' each other.

▶ People tend to share the same tastes – both culinary and cultural.

▶ People tend to expend the same energy in conversation.

▶ People tend to look like their dogs!

Have a think about:

▶ What signals you emanate.

▶ What kind of person you 'bring home'.

▶ How often you say: 'I always seem to meet the same kind of person!' 'I've done it again! Do I never learn?!'

If you think about it, it's remarkable that people find others who are compatible with them, particularly if they have obscure interests or obsessions. It would seem that the subtle signals they put out act as homing devices for those who have similar, or mutually dependent, propensities.

Of course, there are always exceptions ...

→ A note of caution

There is often more than one trigger for a body posture, gesture or movement. These 'rules' are not infallible. If they were, there'd be limited scope for creating drama or mystery and the need for language would almost disappear.

There are also those who are masters or mistresses of disguise. They have acquired sufficient self-knowledge and control to send messages that meet their agenda; sometimes a duplicitous agenda.

→ A checklist for creating impact

Although body language stems from the unconscious, increased self-awareness allows us some control. Once we know what our tendencies are, we can look out for them and train ourselves to do something different.

Bearing in mind the assertiveness essentials of establishing mutual respect and honouring both yours and others' choices, here are some of the approaches you might take to create a positive impact:

▶ Ensure that your body is congruent with your message – what you say is mirrored by the physical channel of communication.

▶ Gather your energy and push it out so that people experience your 'presence'.

▶ Speak clearly and concisely. Know what you mean and mean what you say.

▶ Listen to others carefully so that you can balance the sending and receiving of messages.

▶ Take time. A person responding too fast looks agitated and anxious.

▶ Practice makes perfect!

Summary

This chapter focused on using body language to reinforce your communications and being aware of when it can sabotage you and give away your agenda.

Although body language is largely subconscious, you can manage this important communication tool through being tuned in to your habits and being aware of when they are switched on and switched off. This will give you the option to manage them differently – albeit authentically. A mismatch between your spoken word and your body language breeds mistrust.

Where to next?

The next chapter will pay attention to the important part that listening plays in assertiveness. By listening attentively to what people say and by observing the environment carefully, you will have access to more information than most. This will equip you to preside over situations with greater confidence and speak with assertion.

What have I learnt?

→ What messages do I convey with my body?

_____

_____

_____

_____

_____

_____

_____

→ What 'leakage' do I have that gives my 'real' feelings away?

_____

_____

_____

_____

_____

_____

_____

→ How do I build my first impression with someone I haven't met before? What messages do I convey with my body and demeanour?

_____

_____

_____

_____

_____

_____

_____

→ What do I do to build and demonstrate rapport?

_____

_____

_____

_____

_____

_____

_____

9

Listening assertively

You may think that it's odd to suggest that listening is an element of being assertive. Yet, listening is perhaps one of the sharpest tools in the assertiveness toolkit. It allows you to:

▶ hear new things

▶ gather information that you might otherwise miss

▶ build rapport

▶ establish trusting relationships

▶ create an empathic connection

▶ access your thoughts and feelings accurately

▶ resolve misunderstandings

▶ know what, and how, someone else thinks

▶ walk into the unknown with confidence

▶ identify unique and effective solutions to problems

▶ get a sense of someone's values and beliefs so that you can judge how to strike up a conversation or negotiation.

This list is pretty exhaustive and each item is powerful enough in itself.

The notion of 'active listening' is not new. There are many techniques that you can develop to convey your listening skills and portray your interest in what someone else is saying.

However, let's explore what *non*-active listening is like.

► How many times have you experienced a conversation that miraculously switches to the other person at every opportunity you offer them?

► How many times have you been frustrated by someone's eye wandering around the room to see who else is around?

► How many times have you felt that you were being 'listened to' without being heard?

► How many times have you tried to put across your point of view only to be interrupted, have your sentences finished for you or dismissed with a negative or sarcastic comment?

► How does it feel?

Dismissive	Frustrating	Insulting	Infuriating	Tiresome
?	Irritating	?	Off-putting	Upsetting
Ignorant	?	Disappointing	Lonely	Disenchanting
Disheartening	Trivializing	Arrogant	Unsophisticated	Ingenuous
Artless	Unintelligent	Indifferent	?	Disconcerting
Uncivilized	Discouraging	Depressing	Unattractive	?

Add your own descriptors to fill in the blanks.

In fact, there is nothing positive about not being listened to properly, yet, as an art, we tend to be pretty poor at listening.

Exercise 19

How good are you at listening?

1 **When you want to make a complaint do you...**

   a Deliver your complaint making the assumption it's going to be a battle and jump in when the person you're complaining to appears to argue the counterpoint?

   b Outline your concerns and ask for the other's opinion and thoughts?

   c Look impatient and tap your foot whilst they struggle to establish rapport?

   d Apologize profusely and ask if they think you have a right to complain?

2 **When you're having a disagreement with someone do you...**

   a Make your point forcefully on the assumption that they're going to take an opposing view?

   b Invite them to outline their view so that you can look for the points of agreement?

   c Block any attempt to respond with an 'Oh yeah?' comment to undermine their argument?

   d Say 'You probably know better than me' and acquiesce as soon as possible to keep the peace?

3 **When you're trying to persuade someone of something do you...**

a Ensure that you discharge all your arguments at the outset in the hope that they'll realize the futility of opposing you?

b Declare your intentions and seek the common ground before working on the points of contention?

c Try to demolish their views with a clever quip?

d Tell them that they probably won't want to hear your point of view but if they ask you, you'll let them know what it is?

4 **When you're in a social situation and conversing with someone for the first time do you...**

a Enjoy talking about yourself because it's great to have a captive and 'interested' audience?

b Ask them questions so that you can get to know them a little?

c Listen to them with exaggerated boredom because they don't ask you anything about yourself?

d Listen endlessly and look for an opportunity to escape?

5 **When you go to a new country do you...**

a Declare how different it is from what you're used to and get impatient when you can't get what you want?

b Observe with interest what's going on around you and look for a way in?

c Roll your eyes at some of the extraordinary cultural rituals and think that they're weird?

d Wait to see what happens and where you end up if you just carry on as normal?

By now, you'll probably be able to recognize the four forms of communication spread around the answers.

If you scored mostly 'a', you are likely to be dominating those you encounter and are certainly not listening to them. If this describes you, you are in danger of limiting your knowledge of people and restricting the richness that the world can offer you.

If you scored mostly 'b', you are likely to be listening well. You probably recognize that there is some listening to be done and respect others' perspectives. You may also be interested in hearing these for the inspiration, information or value they can bring to you. However, you may also be kidding yourself. You may be adept at the art of *appearing* to listen but do you *really* do so? Are there gaps in your recollection of a conversation where you've tuned out and been having an imagined conversation of your own? It is quite possible to use the techniques of listening without actually hearing. Check that you don't belong in this camp.

If you scored mostly 'c', you are probably quite defensive and may be reluctant to let down your guard for fear of being questioned or asked to change your views or opinions. You seem to be holding on to what you 'know' and don't want to encounter any challenge to that. It is really hard to learn new things and grow if this is your natural style.

If you scored mostly 'd', you are willing to be carried along by circumstance without resistance. It is as if life is not determined by you, rather, it is determined by chance, good or bad luck. It's probably time to participate more fully in your own fortunes.

If you have a mixture of responses, it would seem that sometimes you're an effective listener and sometimes you're not. If this describes you, take some time to think about what it is that piques your interest and what it is that makes you zone out. Many of us zone out when someone is 'banging' on about something we have no interest in or when they are on their soap box and trying to convince us to change our lives so that we can be more like them.

Neither of these scenarios is particularly appealing as an invitation to listen. However, you might challenge yourself next time you feel yourself about to zone out to try to keep engaged for that little bit longer. Perhaps you could even ask a question to stimulate further – or different – thoughts from the communicator. You may be surprised to hear something that you didn't expect!

Now, ask yourself if you're ever the person who triggers a zone out. Do you tend to get on your hobbyhorse, repeat the same stories or come up with a predictable response? Are you known for your stream of consciousness and for never asking for anyone else's contribution to the conversation? Do you sometimes say 'I'm the only one that's making any effort around here!' Is there a reason for this?

....

Let's now look at how deeply you listen.

→ 1. Listening 'against'

At the most superficial level, you're probably 'listening against' what others are saying. This means that you constantly refer back to what you already know or hold to be true and use this to determine whether or not you receive someone's message or reject it.

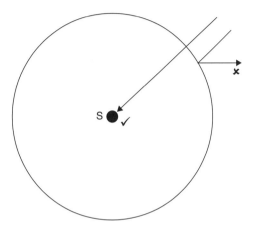

Imagine you're the dot in the middle of the circle above. (S = Self)

Surrounding you is the doughnut that denotes your frame of reference, the frame you use to make your choices – or the lens through which you make sense of the world. This frame is full of your family influences, your societal influences, your values, your beliefs, your prejudices and your assumptions. The information you gather is filtered through this frame and if it accords with what you already believe to be true, you accept it, tick (✓). If it doesn't accord with what you already believe to be true, you reject it, cross (✗). You can see from this diagram that if you always accept things which you already happen to believe and reject those things which you don't happen to believe, you never learn anything new, you never change your opinion and you never grow. This often happens in early adulthood when you believe you've done all your learning and the rest of your time is all about 'doing'.

Most of us spend our time listening 'against'. This is not always a 'bad' thing because, sometimes, we need to be able to tap into what we already know – our knowledge and skills – to deliver a result. We also need to be able to discriminate between new information that is credible to us and new information that is not in order to make decisions. If you never move from this position though, you end up being overly directive and a bit of a 'know it all'!

If you are listening 'against' someone who has a different frame of reference to you, these are the sorts of things you might say and do:

▶ 'You're wrong!'

▶ 'That's not true!'

▶ 'You've not understood properly!'

▶ 'That's not right!'

▶ 'That doesn't make sense!'

You might interrupt a lot, take over the conversation, shout people down and bully them for agreement.

On the other hand, if they see things the way you do, you might say:

▶ 'That's just what I think!'

▶ 'You're absolutely right.'

▶ 'That makes complete sense.'

▶ 'You clearly have a good grasp of the situation.'

▶ 'We clearly see things in the same way.'

And you might build on their comments with enthusiasm and confidence, knowing that they'll receive your wisdom and validate you for being 'right'.

→ 2. Listening 'for'

At the next level of listening, you listen for something new; you are curious about others' lives, ideas and opinions.

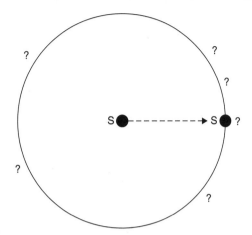

If you imagine yourself as the 'S' again, you have now travelled to the edge of your world and you're looking out, with curiosity. Here, you listen 'for' differences: in experiences, views and thoughts. You are putting yourself to one side, momentarily, and experiencing a new world that you hadn't considered before. This curiosity demands that you ask questions; 'tell me more' questions that often begin with 'who?', 'what?', 'where?', 'when?', 'why?' and 'how?'

These questions begin to reassure people that you're interested in them and *really* listening to them.

If you are listening 'for', these are the things you might say:

▶ 'That's interesting. Tell me more.'

▶ 'I haven't come across that view before. Would you help me understand why you think that?'

▶ 'That's not my experience. Perhaps you'd explain what happened?'

▶ 'Would you tell me why you think that?'

▶ 'What would you say to someone who doesn't share your view?'

▶ 'How could you help me understand this?'

And they might experience you:

▶ keeping eye contact

▶ summarizing what you hear

▶ nodding and saying 'ah ha', 'hmmmm' and 'I see'

▶ asking lots of questions

▶ mirroring their body position and matching their energy.

→ ## 3. Listening with empathy

At the next level, you're interested in others' perspectives. You imagine yourself in their shoes and evoke what you believe would be your feelings or reactions if you were them. At this point, you leave yourself behind and enter the other's world; a world that looks, feels and sounds very different to your own. It is not familiar territory to you so you may find it a bit unnerving. You may also find it a little threatening because in someone else's world, your personal framework may be thrown into a dubious light. By seeing things from another's perspective, you might start questioning your own views and, perhaps, change your mind.

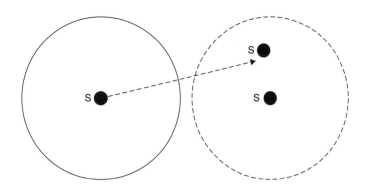

If you were listening empathically, these are the things you might say:

▶ 'Seeing this from your perspective, I can imagine how you must feel.'

▶ 'I've had a similar experience so I understand why you think that.'

▶ 'Oh dear. That must be dreadful.' Or 'How wonderful. That must be amazing!'

And these are the things you might do:

▶ put your arm around their shoulder

▶ keep still and concentrated eye contact

▶ convey your empathy through facial gestures

▶ get into their body space

▶ respond to what they say with appropriate acknowledgement.

Exercise 20

Reflect on what you could do to improve your own listening skills. Tick those that are appropriate. There is space at the bottom of the table to add your own.

What could you do to improve your listening skills?	
Be more interested in someone else's views than your own	
Be curious about others' worlds	
Be able to put yourself aside to give someone else space	
Be able to put your feet in someone else's shoes	
Listen to a child, with whom you are familiar, with renewed curiosity	
Listen as a child, as if for the first time	
Listen to someone who has different expertise to your own	
. . .	
. . .	
. . .	

Try cranking up your listening skills by hearing others at a new level. Start with those you are familiar with. These are the people with whom you are likely to take short cuts in your conversations based upon an unspoken and shared set of values and assumptions. Notice the new things that you learn when you do this.

Summary

In this chapter, the notion of listening deeply has been explored. Listening skills can be demonstrated (or faked) using the classic techniques of: maintaining eye contact, nodding in agreement, summarizing what you've heard, questioning and probing, mirroring body language and matching another's spoken language. Yet, if this is not done genuinely, the communicator can feel as if they've been subject to a technique that is devoid of meaning; an empty experience that is worse than not being listened to in the first place!

Here's an A to J list of the qualities of listening, deeply:

1 **Authenticity** – genuinely being interested in what is being said

2 **Belief** – in your capacity to explore new territory

3 **Curiosity** – about someone else's views and opinions

4 **Discipline** – concentrating on the communicator and bringing your attention back to them whenever it wanders off

5 **Empathy** – the ability to put yourself in someone else's shoes

6 **Focus** – maintaining your intention to listen deeply and placing your attention on the communicator

7 **Glee** – joy in the discovery of something new

8 **Humility** – and a preparedness to suspend judgement, disbelief or prejudice

9 Integrity – a willingness to put your values and ego to one side and let the other take pride of place. Respect for what you hear even if it's miles from what you think or believe

10 **Judgement** – not the same as judging but knowing when to steer someone into new territory so that they don't get stuck in a rut or re-hash 'old stuff' endlessly.

Where to next?

The next chapter is going to explore how you can develop an assertive mindset.

What have I learnt?

→ Generally speaking, how much time do I spend being interested in what others have to say?

_____

_____

_____

_____

_____

_____

_____

→ Putting myself in others' shoes, how would they describe my listening skills?

_____

_____

_____

_____

_____

_____

_____

➔ What realistic goal could I set myself to listen more deeply – and with whom?

_____

_____

_____

_____

_____

_____

_____

➔ How will I maintain – or manage – my listening skills when I'm under pressure?

_____

_____

_____

_____

_____

_____

_____

10

Developing an assertive mindset

In this chapter you will learn:
- ▶ *the power of positive thinking*
- ▶ *how positive your mindset is*
- ▶ *the power of positive affirmations*
- ▶ *how to use creative visualization*
- ▶ *how to create a positive mindset*

This workbook aims to get you 'below the surface' of assertive behaviour. It's not just a matter of applying techniques to simulate assertiveness, but of becoming assertive from the inside out.

The last chapter focused on developing assertive listening skills. By drawing upon 'real' information rather than assumptions, you are in a position to understand what you're dealing with and identify the tools that will help you do so to best effect. By listening deeply, too, you'll be able to challenge some of your formerly held beliefs and freshen your thinking.

If you are to learn and grow new skills, it is important that you let something go. No doubt, you've met people who stopped growing at a certain age and who are now so hardened to new information and experiences, that they're living a kind of 'ground-hog' existence, where they go round the same behavioural loops over and over again – and suffer the consequences.

This chapter will look at how you condition your mind to think assertively and to demand assertive behaviours of yourself. In this way, your habits will change along with your relationships, which will become more grounded in an agreed reality and more authentic.

You've probably heard of positive thinking and positive affirmations.

Positive thinking is a predisposition of the mind; an attitude that is self-reinforcing and generative. In other words, it has a 'going places' momentum that makes things happen.

When you think positively:

► Rather than seeing the problems, you see the opportunities in a situation. Rather than being pessimistic, you take an optimistic view.

► You look for the joy and pleasure in life rather than the misfortune.

► Your glass is half full, rather than half empty.

► You are curious and have energy for new experiences.

► You create positivity around yourself.

AND:

► You are more likely to be happy ...

► ... and achieve your ambitions and aspirations.

Exercise 21

How positive is your attitude?

Look at the scales below and rank your positivity from 1–10 by circling the number that represents your position between the two extremes. (1 = Low and 10 = High)

When you travel to somewhere you haven't been before, what are your thoughts and feelings?

| I dread going to new places because I don't know what I'll find – and it's bound to be troublesome | 1 | 2 | 3 | 4 | 5 | 6 | 7 | 8 | 9 | 10 | I love the unexpected and unknown aspects of a new place and get a thrill from the adventure |

When you meet a new person, what are your thoughts and feelings?

| I'm not good at meeting new people. It takes me ages to get to know and trust them | 1 | 2 | 3 | 4 | 5 | 6 | 7 | 8 | 9 | 10 | I really enjoy meeting new people. You never know what you're going to find! |

When someone asks you if they can have a private word, what are your thoughts and feelings?

| They're bound to complain about what I've said or done and leave me feeling bad | 1 | 2 | 3 | 4 | 5 | 6 | 7 | 8 | 9 | 10 | I look forward to finding out what's on their mind. It could be to my advantage |

When you start a new job, what are your thoughts and feelings?

I'm worried that people will find out what I'm not capable of and not want to work with me. Then I'll lose my job!	1	2	3	4	5	6	7	8	9	10	I like learning new things and see this as an opportunity to develop my professional skills and meet new people

When you enter a new personal relationship, what are your thoughts and feelings?

I wonder how long it will be before they go off me and leave me for someone else!	1	2	3	4	5	6	7	8	9	10	They should be so lucky! Now I can have some fun!

When you're invited to do something you haven't done before, what are your thoughts and feelings?

I'm wondering how I can get out of it as I'm sure I won't enjoy myself	1	2	3	4	5	6	7	8	9	10	I'm delighted that someone is expanding my life experience

If you have a challenging experience, what are your thoughts and feelings?

I think it's a pattern and that it will continue for the rest of the day – and it usually does!	1	2	3	4	5	6	7	8	9	10	I relegate it to the 'trash can' in my mind and look forward to something good happening

When you look at the position of your marks on the scales, what do you notice?

If you tend to place your mark towards the higher end of the scale, it would seem that you do, indeed, have a positive mindset and probably enjoy the fruits of this in terms of your relationships and new experiences. You might even say that you feel 'lucky' as life tends to smile upon you.

If your marks are clustered in the middle of the scale, the jury is out! What prevents you from making your marks higher up the scale? Do you feel that you'll be disappointed if you're over-optimistic or 'over-enthusiastic' about life so you guard yourself a little? (But not too much because you don't want to put off those good things by being negative.) Does this indicate that you're not taking full responsibility for your life?

If you veer towards the lower end of the scale with your marks, it would seem that you take a rather gloomy view of life and that your expectations tend to be negative. Are you the sort of person who, if they stub their toe as they get out of bed in the morning, think that the whole day is going to follow the same trend? Do you hear yourself saying: 'It's obviously going to be 'that' sort of day!' after a couple of these minor instances? Do you notice the 'bad' things and ignore the 'good'? How often do you count your blessings?

If your marks are scattered, you may be driven by the situation, or by your past memories of things that have gone well or poorly. By using the past as a measure for the future, you may prevent a positive change occurring because you never let new possibilities exceed your past experiences. You may even become superstitious, believing that the repetition of your experiences is contingent upon something that you do, or don't do.

Ask yourself:

► What would it take to drive your marks up to the positive end of the scale?

► What will you do differently next time you're in a negative situation that you've encountered before? Make notes in the box below.

| | | |
| | | |

If you have found that you have a positive mindset, you probably have an equally positive inner dialogue. For those of you who do not have such a positive mindset, positive affirmations may help you move into a state of positivity.

→ Positive affirmations

Positive affirmations are statements you make to yourself repeatedly until you believe them to be true. Then, you can act as if they are true, thereby, reinforcing their truth. The repetition is important because your positive self-talk has to over-ride the myriad negative statements (or negative affirmations) that you've already made to yourself over the years.

Messages that we give ourselves continually carve a groove in our brain which acts as an easy conduit for other similar messages. These similar messages flow along this groove as the path of least resistance and increase its depth, rather like a river cutting through a mountain range. The longer the river travels the same path, the deeper it becomes and the harder it is to change its route.

Positive affirmations are designed to 'speak' to the unconscious mind and motivate you to achieve a particular outcome or goal. When you engage the unconscious mind, it works on your behalf, seeking to prove the validity of what it is you have put there.

Exercise 22

Think about a few goals that you'd like to reach in, say, the next ten years. (A timescale is helpful because it focuses your attention on reaching the goal. If you just say 'one day', your goal will always be one day away!) These goals may be related to your work, your body or your personal aspirations. Make them ambitious but realistic.

Also, couch them in terms that enable you to know when you've reached them. For instance: 'I'm going to get better at communicating' is not a 'good' goal because you don't know what 'better' is like and you don't know when you'll do it by. 'In the next year, I'm going to become assertive enough to enter a room where I know no-one and speak to five people' is a 'better' goal.

Write down your goals below.

These are the goals I'd like to reach in the next ten years:

	Professional	Personal
1.		
2.		
3.		

You will be using these goals to devise your positive affirmations later.

Below are the attributes of a positive affirmation:

- ▶ They are positive!
- ▶ They are about you. They are not about anyone else. 'I want my boss to like me!' is **NOT** a positive affirmation. It's a hope. 'I am growing in professional competence and effectiveness' is a positive affirmation.
- ▶ They are spoken of as if they already exist. For instance: 'I am confident and capable'; 'I am healthy and fit'; 'I feel good about myself;' If you put them in the future, you'll always be chasing them.
- ▶ They are succinct. They don't ramble on for hours telling a convoluted story.
- ▶ There is no condition attached to their truth. You would **NOT** say: 'When I lose weight, I will feel good about myself.' You would say: 'I am losing weight and I feel good about myself.'
- ▶ They are beliefs you really want to hold so there is some passion attached to their repetition.
- ▶ They are repeated many times over, every day. (Perhaps in front of a mirror so that you get the visual channel of this form of communication.)
- ▶ You really believe them!

Exercise 23

Concoct your own positive affirmations in relation to one or two of your goals above:

My goal	My positive affirmation

→ Two notes of caution

Positive affirmations are not a panacea for all ills. Although they should support a stretch goal, this goal must also fall within the bounds of possibility. If you're over 250lbs and you have a goal to be a sprinter, you might want to spend some time dwelling upon the likelihood of you achieving this. Are you kidding yourself or are you really seeking to achieve this goal? If you are unrealistic in the way you set your goal, you will only succeed in achieving a sense of failure, which does nothing for your self-esteem. Perhaps having a shorter-term goal would be a good start in this instance. Then you could concoct a really supportive positive affirmation such as: 'I am losing weight and getting fit!'

If, however, you create a secondary affirmation that is negative, you will undermine the effect of the positive affirmation. For example, if your positive affirmation is: 'I communicate assertively and can say 'No!' at will' but inside you're thinking 'Like hell I do!' you will nullify the power of the positive affirmation. You must learn to resist the temptation to sabotage your efforts. Just the smallest seed of doubt can undermine your positive affirmations so go for gold and believe them wholeheartedly.

→ A final note

If you want to feel positive about yourself, do something that you're good at and remind yourself of the many talents you have.

CREATIVE VISUALIZATION

Another way of creating a positive mindset is to use your imagination to envisage a different world for yourself. Creative visualization can also be a positive affirmation but instead of it being spoken, it is seen in the mind's eye.

In Chapter 3, creative visualization was suggested as a technique for dealing with an aggressive person. If you imagine yourself dealing with someone in your preferred way, you become familiar with these new behaviours and they feel quite natural to you when you need to draw upon them.

Practitioners of NLP (Neuro-Linguistic Programming) know that we tend to make things bigger in our minds if we hold a specific fear. People who suffer from arachnophobia tend to magnify the size of spiders in their mind. What others may see as a tiny spider, appears as a massive image in the mind's eye of the person with the phobia and, the more powerful the fear, the larger the image. This makes it difficult for them to cope when they see one. Contrastingly, if you shrink the size of something that you fear in your mind, your fear diminishes in similar proportion. This is the art of creative visualization.

Creative visualization can be used in many different ways. You can use it to:

▶ Envisage goals that you want to achieve.

▶ Rehearse presentations that you need to give or meetings that you need to hold.

▶ Work out how you want to encounter someone you find challenging.

▶ Find answers to problems you're trying to find solutions for.

▶ Resolving worrying issues.

▶ Access your subconscious wisdom.

Exercise 24

Here's how you do it:

1 Find a place where you can be quiet and undisturbed for about ten to fifteen minutes.

2 Spend a little while getting comfortable and relaxing so that there are no physiological or psychological obstacles in your way.

3 Some people like to close their eyes so that there is nothing to distract them from their visualization.

4 You might use a positive affirmation to get yourself started. Something like: 'I trust my mind to give me the answers'; 'Ideas are flowing from my mind;' 'I am ready to tap my natural creativity and wisdom.' (You're telling your subconscious what you want from it when you do this.)

5 Focus on the problem, issue or purpose of your visualization. Conjure up the image that represents your need or wish. For instance, it might be a question that you're seeking an answer to. See it as you might a film on a screen and allow yourself a period of free association where you follow the lead of your mind into new territory. Don't fight it. Even if it feels a bit 'off beat', indulge your mind's desires and see where it leads you.

6 Try not to judge what you're witnessing. Your mind works in images and these will contain messages for you. If you argue with the content of these images using your rational brain, you'll destroy the potential messages they hold for you.

7 When you've finished, open your eyes and rest them on something tangible.

8 Write down anything that occurred to you during your visualization and attend to any new thoughts that bubble up throughout the day. Your mind will continue to work on your material until you tell it to stop!

....

Some people prefer to do guided visualizations. For this, they are taken on an imaginary journey by someone who talks them through the process, step-by-step. If you're new to visualization, this may be a good introduction for you. You can ask someone to sit with you and direct your experience or you can get one of the many CDs that contain guided visualizations or meditations.

Really, what you're doing when you do a visualization is pushing your logical brain out of the way whilst you access your creative brain. This is where the solutions to knotty problems reside. Make a habit of doing this so that you can turn to this technique at will.

Summary

In this chapter, the means of creating a positive mindset was explored. If we expect the best outcome as we go through our day there's a better chance that we'll notice the things that go well. It's like when you want to buy a certain make of car, because it's in your mind, you notice it everywhere. So, if you condition your mind to notice the positives, they'll be everywhere too!

Creative visualization was also offered as a technique for 'seeing' solutions to problems or answers to questions. By spending some time in your imagination, you can access what you know from a different vantage point. It is rare that you'll leave such an exercise without having benefited from it, especially if you enter the experience with a positive mindset!

Where to next?

In the next chapter, we're going to focus on persuading, negotiating and managing conflict. This is hard territory for the non-assertive person who often believes that others' rights hold supremacy over their own.

What have I learnt?

→ How would I describe my ability to control my mind and prevent it from 'taking off' on its own fantasy?

_____

_____

_____

_____

_____

_____

_____

→ What positive affirmations will serve my aspirations and personal growth?

_____

_____

_____

_____

_____

_____

_____

→ How will I prevent self-sabotage by not *really* believing in my ability to change?

_____

_____

_____

_____

_____

_____

_____

→ Which part of me is doing the self-observation and which part of me is being observed? When I'm watching myself act, who is the more authentic, the watcher or the one being watched?

_____

_____

_____

_____

_____

_____

_____

11 *Influencing, negotiating and managing conflict*

In this chapter you will learn:
- ▶ *what kind of influencer you are*
- ▶ *the advantages and disadvantages of the different influencing styles*
- ▶ *how to use the influencing planning sheet*
- ▶ *how to prepare for, and conduct, a win-win negotiation*
- ▶ *how to use the negotiation planning sheet*
- ▶ *how to deal with difficult people*

The last chapter argued for a positive mindset as a means of accessing a more assertive style of communication. By having positive disposition, you are more likely to bring the best outcomes to yourself.

This chapter will build on your developing assertiveness skills and take you into the difficult territory where you seek to preside over a situation and bring it to a satisfactory conclusion from your own perspective. This might sound a bit like a win-lose dynamic, which is the counterpoint to assertiveness, but there are times when your goals can be satisfied without the other party feeling that they've lost.

→ Influencing

When you aim to influence someone, you may be met with resistance or you may be 'pushing on an open door', depending on some practical factors. We are much more likely to be influenced by those:

- ▶ who we know, like and trust

- ▶ who hold similar values to our own

- ▶ to whom we owe a favour or a debt of gratitude

- ▶ in authority

- ▶ who have already influenced many and, therefore, represent a popular view

- ▶ who fit our physical stereotype of attractiveness and trustworthiness.

We also tend to be more easily influenced if something is thought to be scarce or if there's a chance we may be personally disadvantaged, or at a loss, if we don't succumb to the influential arguments.

Exercise 25

What kind of influencer are you? There are many influencing tactics that are available to be used. Have a think about the ones that you adopt most frequently and whether they are serving you.

Look at the scale between the opposites. Circle the position that you think most accurately describes your influencing style.

1. Logical vs Friendly

I tend to use reason and logical arguments supported by facts, figures and statistics. I like to be concrete and objective in my influencing approach	1	2	3	4	5	6	7	8	9	10	I like to make a personal connection and build common ground so that I can influence through a friendly relationship. I like to be subjective and tap emotions

2. Visual vs a 'Trade-off'

I like to paint a picture of the future so that people can see what the possibilities are for them. I can make it rich and evocative so that they can build enthusiasm and commitment. This is a 'pull' strategy	1	2	3	4	5	6	7	8	9	10	*I like to use people's desire to get something for nothing by offering them something desirable in exchange for their commitment to my agenda. This is a 'push' strategy.*

3. Referential vs Persistent

I like to use the fact that other credible or similar people have been influenced and that it is therefore safe to be influenced as they'll join this growing community of like-minded people.	1	2	3	4	5	6	7	8	9	10	*I just keep going until I've influenced someone with my arguments, and I'll use whichever ones I think will work. I'm pretty persistent and don't give up until I get what I want*

Have a think about:

▶ What your most common influencing challenge is.

▶ What you notice about your style and whether it serves you well.

▶ Whether you stick consistently to one style and find yourself down the same alley each time you make an attempt to influence someone.

▶ Whether the adoption of another style might increase your effectiveness.

Below are the advantages and disadvantages of each style. These descriptions may help you think about how influence others and whether there is more you can do to increase your effectiveness.

Influencing others

Style and definition	Advantages	Disadvantages
Logical (Facts, Figures, Statistics, Objective, Impartial. Appeals to the rational mind.)	Trades on certainty and security. Perceived to minimize risk. It is a 'grounded' approach that conveys reason and objectivity.	It is not mediated by instinct, intuition or emotion so can seem cold and inflexible. May be seen as lacking in creativity.
Friendly (Making connections, listening well and empathizing. Taking a positive view)	A spirit of openness and trust is generated leading to an exchange of ideas and eventual 'buy-in'. The person being influenced feels part of the outcome.	Can be seen as a little insipid if the influencer's views are held back in the interests of building a friendly relationship. May appear 'soft'.
Visual (Painting a rich picture of the future, helping people see desirable outcomes and benefits. Conveys 'we're in this exciting adventure together'.)	It generates enthusiasm and provides energy and momentum to reach a future aspiration. It taps into people's desires and emotions.	It may be seen as the triumph of fantasy over realism. Could be perceived as 'flakey' or risky because facts may not be emphasized.
A 'Trade-off' ('You scratch my back and I'll scratch yours', trading, striking deals)	Generates a sense of reciprocal exchange and hooks in the person being influenced. Can be seen as a fair exchange.	Used inelegantly, it could be seen as blackmail or a way of avoiding an unacceptable loss. Might be seen as manipulative and threatens trust.
Referential (Referring to credible others, rules and regulations or organizations to build a case)	Conveys the impression of being connected to an important network. Being the mouthpiece for those in authority can be impressive and suggest power, which is often seen as attractive to align to. It can demolish counter-arguments.	Can been seen as coercive by seemingly, diminishing choice. Assumes someone's susceptibility to authority which, if not present, leaves the argument bare. The influencer might be seen as weak for not taking responsibility for their own arguments.

Persistent (Presenting and re-presenting arguments until they have been accepted)	The influencer is seen as confident and straightforward. They say what they mean and mean what they say. This is an uncomplicated style that allows for direct challenge and debate.	The influencer can be seen as bullying and dogmatic. As a result of adopting a more autocratic tactic, the influencer be outmanoeuvred by those with quick wit or greater levels of subtlety.

All these influencing approaches aim to achieve a specific objective, one where the person being influenced co-operates with person doing the influencing.

Assertiveness is a genuine win-win approach that takes the best of each of these styles and builds common ground where the outcome is negotiated between the two parties.

→ Plan your influencing approach

Do you have an influencing challenge looming? If so, try using the planning sheet below to decide how you're going to approach it and which tactic you're going to adopt. If it's one that's not so natural to you, how are you going to prepare yourself? You may need to find someone for whom the approach you choose is quite normal. They can then talk you through it or, perhaps, role-play the influencing conversation so that you can get used to the sound of yourself doing something different.

INFLUENCING PLANNING SHEET

(Customize this planning sheet to meet your needs.)

Position	Information		Resources/Activity
My influencing goal is:			
My counterpart's position is likely to be:			
My 'fall back' position is:			
What I know about them:	Position/ attitude		
	Context		
	Values		
	History		
	Aspirations		
	Needs		
My influencing tactic will be:			
What information do I need to back up my position? (Facts, figures, anecdotes, examples, stories, others' views...)			

When should the meeting take place?		
Where should the meeting take place?		
Who do I need to speak to beforehand?		
Who else needs to be involved in the meeting?		

Once you've had your chosen influencing conversation, write down your thoughts and experiences and think about what went well and what you could have done differently. This will ensure that nothing of your learning is lost and will go towards building your aptitude.

→ Negotiation

Much has been written about effective negotiation techniques and they range both widely and deeply. For this reason, it is not possible to enter a full exploration of the topic here, and it would only repeat what's already widely written. However, by clipping the peaks of good win-win practice, and by adopting an assertive style for your negotiations, you will be more in control and able to bring the exchange to a satisfactory conclusion. Win-win negotiations allow:

- ▶ trust to be built
- ▶ relationships to be maintained in the longer term
- ▶ the most effective solution to be reached
- ▶ a fair outcome for all parties
- ▶ access to additional/new information
- ▶ unexpected opportunities to emerge
- ▶ everyone to feel that they've 'won'

HOW TO PREPARE FOR A WIN-WIN NEGOTIATION

Preparation: When entering a negotiation, you need to think carefully about what you want to achieve, both in terms of the immediate outcome and the long term gains and benefits that might spring from it. It is rare that you can enter a negotiation and conduct it to best effect without preparation. Although some people do like to approach negotiations in a spontaneous and instinctive manner, the outcome will be more uncertain. In your preparation, you need to consider:

► Who you'll be negotiating with. Consider their style and values and think about how you can connect with them.

► Who holds the power and what the other party's expectations are about the outcome.

► What you're aiming to achieve.

► What 'price' you're prepared to pay for it.

► What concessions you're prepared to make.

► What the best alternative to meeting your aspirations would be.

► At what point you'd walk away.

► The context in which it is being conducted (Is it a one-off negotiation? Is it contentious? Does it have multiple stakeholders?)

► The timing of the negotiation. How long will it take and is the timing of its occurrence critical.

► How important it is to maintain the relationship(s) in the long term.

► What the consequences to your agreement will be.

Preamble: Having covered the territory thoroughly, your mind will need to turn to the preamble. For this, you'll need to consider:

► Whether there is a need for communication or an information exchange that needs to take place beforehand. Perhaps there is some documentation that has to be prepared in readiness for the negotiation, for instance.

► Whether there are relationships that need to be formed, cultivated, canvassed, nurtured or maintained before you enter the negotiation

► Where the negotiation is going to take place. For instance: Will you host it on your premises? Will you be a guest on theirs? Will it take place in a neutral location?

► Who will need to be present and what roles they will occupy. For instance: Does it need to be witnessed? Does it need to be recorded? Should experts be present?

Entering the negotiation: Think about your mindset and your feelings before you enter the negotiation and, having prepared for the negotiation materially, prepare yourself emotionally by:

► checking your assumptions about the other party/parties

► ensuring that you have a win-win mindset

► determining to keep calm and if things go awry, to develop a strategy to keep yourself on track

► being curious about their position and prepared to ask lots of questions.

During the negotiation: When you're involved in the negotiation, try to be conscious of your responses and reactions to the other. Sit on your own shoulder, like a 'mini me', and observe yourself objectively. Notice when you recoil from the person you're negotiating with and also notice when your feelings start to peak, positively or negatively. These are signals that you're getting emotionally involved (perhaps your values are being compromised) and you need to exercise some self-discipline and self-control. If you're aiming for a win-win solution, it is contingent upon you doing certain things really well. For instance, you need to:

▶ Seek the points of mutual agreement or understanding. You may be surprised to find that here are more areas of convergence than divergence. You can then focus on the remaining points only.

▶ Agree any points of acceptable compromise and get them off the table.

▶ Listen curiously and ask lots of open questions to elicit as much information as possible on points of contention. Explore ideas, options and alternatives.

▶ Be empathic and notice what's going on for the other person or people in the negotiation. You can give them feedback in the form: 'I get the impression that you're uncomfortable with that solution. May I ask what's on your mind?' This will establish and then reinforce your intention to establish a reciprocal connection.

▶ If something unexpected happens that you don't have an immediate answer for, be prepared to take a 'time out' to think about things.

Some technical points to help you: When you're planning your approach, there are some advantageous strategies that you could adopt (without entering a win-lose battle!)

▶ *Make your offer first.* When you make your offer first, you 'anchor' the figure that you're prepared to honour – or the position that you're prepared to take. The other party will generally deviate from this within a margin of acceptability. So, if you have an idea that you want, say, £10,000 from them and they have an idea that they want to pay £3,000 to, you need to get your figure in first – you need to 'anchor' it – so that they don't feel able to deviate from your figure by such a large amount. They may, instead, make a counter offer of £8,000, which is much better than you trying to raise them from their £3,000 aspiration.

► *Use 'avoidance of risk' to couch your arguments.* People tend to be persuaded more readily by the possibility of avoiding something 'bad' rather than the promise of getting something 'good'. Our fear of losing out and leaving ourselves exposed is much more compelling than the possibility of gaining an advantage. For example, perhaps you buy a lottery ticket because your fear of losing out should your numbers come up are greater than the lure of the prize?

Concluding the negotiation: Once your negotiation has taken place and you're ready to depart, think about how you want to leave things:

► Sum up and agree the outcome

► Agree the paperwork to complete and when this will be done by

► Agree next steps/follow-up

► Thank the party/parties and depart with a good grace

Avoid:

► threats/blackmail/coercion

► intransigence or having non-negotiable points

► assumptions/stereotypes/fantasies about the other's intentions

► bullying/aggressive tactics

► bluffs, one-upmanship or brinkmanship

► inauthenticity

► being revengeful or vengeful

► fury/anger/over-emotional responses

► being dogged and overly logical. The rational approach is not effective when emotions are engaged.

Here is a planning sheet to help you capture all the elements of your forthcoming negotiation:

Planning stage	Considerations	Information/Actions	
Preparation	People involved		
	Purpose of the negotiation		
	Position	Ours:	Theirs:
	Desired outcome		
	Best alternative to the desired outcome		
	Compromises/Concessions		
Preamble	Information – what information needs to be shared beforehand?		
	People – who will be involved and how do these relationships need to be nurtured?		
	Place – where will the negotiation take place?		

Entering the negotiation	What assumptions are being made?		
	What is the negotiating strategy? (Win-Win, Win-lose)		
During the negotiation	Look for:	Points of mutual understanding	
		Points of agreement	
		Areas of contention	
	Look out for:	Listening	
		Questioning	
		Giving feedback	
Concluding the negotiation	Sum up agreement		
	Agree follow-up documentation		
	Agree next steps		
	Conclude the negotiation		

→ Dealing with difficult people and managing heightened emotions

Finally, in this chapter, the issue of dealing with difficult and angry people will be considered.

Generally, we find people who confront us with their frustrations threatening and they trigger that familiar 'fight', 'flight', 'freeze' or 'roll over' response. What they're trying to do is stick their personal angst on everyone else, presumably, in the hope that they can rid themselves of it completely – or at least ensure that others have to experience the same fury so that they don't have to go around feeling worse than everyone else!

What's your natural response to difficult people?

▶ Fight: I get defensive and give them as good as I get!

▶ Flight: I disappear as fast as possible to get away from the problem.

▶ Freeze: I can't think of anything to say or do so I just stand there!

▶ Roll over: I do whatever I can to appease them.

Whatever is your natural response, there are ways you can manage yourself in these situations that may help you feel more in control.

Firstly, it's important to remember that *it is not about you*. It is all about them! Although they will be projecting their difficulties onto you, it is because they don't have the strategies to deal with them for themselves. They probably feel out of control and vulnerable and feel that they have to fight to get their needs met. Indeed, the difficulty they're expressing is likely to equate to the difficulty they're feeling. You could try putting your feet in their shoes to see how it 'feels' to be them. This might enable you to respond in an appropriately assertive way. You might say something like: 'I understand you feel upset about this but this is not winning me over. I'd really like it if you explained to me what's going on.'

Secondly, anger is just pent up energy looking for somewhere to express itself. If you meet anger with anger, you just make it burn more ferociously, like oxygenating a fire. As long as it isn't physical and you don't need to rescue yourself, try eliminating the oxygen and *don't respond*.

Thirdly, don't be drawn into the issue of who's right and who's wrong. *Avoid a battle of egos*. It will rarely get you anywhere. Try to distance yourself from the arguments, which are pretty irrelevant at this time, and focus on diffusing the emotion. You can do this by distancing yourself (physically or emotionally) and letting the difficult person exhaust their emotions, or by acknowledging their feelings and giving them a way out, such as an offer to sit down and talk about it openly. You'll need to judge the correct level of response.

Fourthly, *use an assertive style of communication* to demonstrate that you respect yourself (as well as them) and that you won't subject yourself to any form of abuse. You might say something like: 'I can see that you're really frustrated but I'm not going to stay here any longer. I would, however, be willing to have a conversation with you later on.' (Being assertive allows you to choose which style of communication will serve you best. There may be times of extremis when a different style is called upon – 'roll over', walk away or retaliate.)

Most of us have our pet frustrations and get drawn in to expressing them when they are triggered. Usually, they are based upon a belief, that may be unverifiable, or a behaviour, that reminds us of something from the past. Expressing frustration for either of these reasons is futile. Facts that are unverifiable and memories that lie in the past have no substance to them. For these reasons, the expression of frustrations is merely hot air. Through self-awareness, you can begin to recognize these triggers and your typical reaction to them. Rather than fight battles that have no substance, then, you can choose your battles thereby gaining some control over your emotional life.

Summary

This chapter has covered that tricky territory where two people come up against each other with different values and different agendas. By being aware of your typical behavioural responses and susceptibilities, you will be able to decide how you want to conduct yourself. Self-mastery is the outcome of developing assertiveness skills and you're well on the way to developing this, having reached this stage of the workbook.

Where to next?

In the next chapter, you will be asked to think about how you're going to sustain your development and keep your resolve. By thinking about how you enter and deal with personal transition, you'll be able to discover where you are on your journey and how to resource yourself to reach the outcome you want.

What have I learnt?

→ What frame of mind am I in when I am at my most influential?

_____

_____

_____

_____

_____

_____

_____

→ What is my approach to finding common ground with those I am influencing and how effective am I at doing it?

_____

_____

_____

_____

_____

_____

_____

→ How do I know when I've encountered someone with whom I share my values compared to those with whom I don't?

_____

_____

_____

_____

_____

_____

→ In the interests of a successful negotiation, how do I 'bracket' or factor out my values, and what does that feel like?

_____

_____

_____

_____

_____

_____

_____

12 *Transition and change*

In this chapter you will learn:
► *the nature of transition and change*
► *the different stages that we encounter in our transformational learning*
► *what can derail our learning*
► *how to resource yourself as you enter your own transformational path*
► *the rewards innate in the process of your growth – confidence and joy!*

Learning new behaviours changes the dynamics of our world.

People get used to the way we are, warts and all, and conspire to hold us in that familiar place because they've learned how to deal with us when we're there. When we change, it throws them into confusion and they have to think about what their new reactions to us mean for them and what choices they wish to make in order to deal with us. Many will try to persuade us back into our familiar 'old' behaviours. It might start as a jokey comment; 'What's got into you all of a sudden??!!'. This is designed to cajole us back to the place where the 'rules' of engagement were well-known and where their interests were served. Humour is a great tool for masking discomfort, but our counterparts are likely to get more serious when they see our determination to make the transition into greater self-assertion and higher levels of self-determination.

The reluctance to see us make this transition indicates more about them that it does about us. The reason for this is that it compels them to notice things about themselves that may be unpalatable to them. (They used to be able to manipulate or control us to fill the gaps in their capabilities or confidence. Now that this avenue is no longer available to them, they have to find someone else to serve their purposes or acknowledge that they're lacking in certain ways.) Indeed, they may dislike us for bringing about their self-realization and do everything they can to keep things running as they were, with us responding in our usual way and them gaining in their usual way! Eventually, when they see your resolve, they'll take themselves off and look for others to occupy the space that was once reserved for you.

Without the loss of friends or acquaintances, transition and change is bewildering enough, but when our relationships are jeopardized because of a goal we're choosing to pursue, we may think twice about our willingness to travel the course. Especially when, we might argue, at such a time, it is our friends and acquaintances that get us through. However, you can't change one thing – your communication style – without changing myriad other things and, on our quest for self-assertion, those closest to us may be the casualties.

If you've learned to say 'No!', for instance, you also have to deal with people's reaction to your ability to say 'No!' As we have already pointed out, you may lose favour with some of your, so called, friends because you're not meeting their agenda any more. (Good!)

However, this knock on effect can feel confusing and evoke feelings of loss – of our friends and of ourselves. For this reason, many of us try to reverse back into our old habits for the sake of preserving what is familiar to us, even if it causes us pain. But, the transitional path, once embarked upon, is unbending and tends to keep us in thrall to the end. For, after the first step, we cannot 'un-have' our insights or 'un-know' our truths.

Let's examine what this transitional process looks like.

The following staged process has been identified from a study of a dozen people who reflected upon their journeys of personal transition and change.

STAGE 1 – IGNORANCE IS BLISS!

This is how we are before the scales drop from our eyes and we see the consequences of perpetuating our behaviours. This is the place where everything is as it has always been and we haven't really come to grips with the impact of our behavioural or communication style.

STAGE 2 – TRIGGER

This is usually quite a painful wake up call. It may be a shock or a crisis that you face that makes it impossible for you to continue to deny your 'stuff'. People may have tried to draw your attention to your behavioural susceptibilities and idiosyncrasies in the past but it is amazing how good we are at dismissing or denying information about ourselves that we find unappealing.

In terms of your impetus to develop assertiveness skills, your trigger may have been something like missing a great job, losing a good relationship (or being compelled into a poor relationship), leaving yourself exposed to criticism or being used to do someone's dirty work for them. Indeed, it may be that your lack of assertiveness disadvantaged you to such an extent that you could no longer allow yourself to continue in that vein. Whatever the trigger, it seems that you collected your determination and set off on the path to becoming assertive.

STAGE 3 – REVELATION

This is the point when the full extent of your challenge hits you; it is the 'ah ha' moment when you begin to understand how the consequences you've experienced are related to your actions, which are under your control. People tend to look back and see that they have been repeating the same patterns for a long time. They may even have built a reputation on these patterns, perhaps being known as a 'Yes man', 'An easy touch' or a 'Cold bitch'. These are hard labels to come to terms with. To perpetuate these behaviours now would be a deliberate act of denial and you would be choosing to keep yourself smaller than you are.

STAGE 4 – DISINTEGRATING

Common to all models of transition are feelings of confusion, perhaps even despair, as reliance on your old behaviours is shed in favour of the new. It's as if you're leaving familiar ground, wantonly, in order to enter uncharted and challenging territory where you're bound to have to live on your wits and fight a few battles, before finally reaching your destination. The promise, by whom or by what is not clear, is that the different landscape of your destination is somehow better than the landscape you left behind. But this is a matter of faith and there are bound to be times, of which you are now horribly aware, that you wish you'd never set out! And, unfortunately, you probably feel at your least able at the very moment you'd like to feel fully resourced! Your old talents, skills and behaviours no longer serve you and everything feels a bit clunky because you haven't yet found or perfected your deeper capabilities. However, once you've started, the only option is to travel boldly. If you hesitate or try to turn back, you'll only cause yourself more confusion and more discomfort.

The qualities of courage and tenacity are undoubtedly needed during this stage of the process.

This is not the time to make sense of things. That comes later. Rather, it is a time to experience the 'undoing' phase of your transition, even though you may experience it as unpleasant. However, as you'll probably want to get away from this stage as fast as possible you may be tempted to start grabbing for solutions. Because of this, it is helpful to distract yourself by doing other things.

(It is worth mentioning, perhaps, that there are some people who LOVE change. They love the uncertainties, the new possibilities and the unknown adventure that is waiting for them. All these things excite and delight them and they become habitual change seekers with a 'Devil may care' attitude. These are not the most sympathetic types if you're struggling with your own transition!)

STAGE 5 – FINDING YOUR VOICE AND BEING HEARD

Whilst you're in the wilderness of your own transition you need to find someone who you can talk to, and who will listen to you patiently and sympathetically, as you express your feelings and experiences. They take the important role of a witness as they watch you pick out a thought, turn it over in your head, and find a new place to put it back. By speaking out in this way, you make something that feels quite *subjective*, more tangible and *objective*. Objectivity gives you a different perspective that enables you to make some decisions about how you want to take things forward.

Being validated at this time is also important so find someone who is on your side to make you feel better about yourself whilst you muse.

STAGE 6 – MAKING SENSE OF IT ALL

By stepping back and looking at your transitional process objectively, you will be able to recognize some themes and gain some understanding. You may examine some cause and effect linkages that illuminate the source of your communication style, whether it be reticence, aggression or a combination of the two. By examining past in this way and locating the source of your style you'll be able to think about what you want to take forward, what you want to shed and what you want to replace. By the end of this stage, you will have the information and the inspiration you need to choose a new approach.

STAGE 7 – CONTROLLING

In the language of developmental psychologists, growth leads to increasing levels of autonomy. The inclination to be loved and defined by another is replaced by a desire and ability to define oneself. This is the time when you start asserting yourself, making your choices and getting what you need. You become the arbiter of your own fortunes and it feels authentic and self-determining. The rewards of being true to oneself are many, including increased confidence and happiness.

Beware, however, of being overly exuberant. There's nothing worse than someone who is over-playing their 'rights'. People who display too much assertion can easily become self-obsessed and aggressive.

STAGE 8 – INTEGRATING

At this stage all the past learning is drawn together, and all the wisdom that has been accumulated, is mined in the process of self-actualizing. According to Maslow, self-actualization is 'an episode in which the powers of the person come together in a particularly efficient and intensely enjoyable way, and in which he or she is more integrated and less spilt, more open for experience, more idiosyncratic, more perfectly expressive or spontaneous, more fully functioning, more creative, more humorous, more ego-transcending, more independent of his or her lower needs, etc. He or she becomes, in these episodes, more truly him/herself, more perfectly actualizing in his/her potentialities, closer to the core of his/her Being, more fully human.'

In essence, you are beginning to find firm ground through self-understanding and the different parts of you are all working together in harmony.

STAGE 9 – LETTING GO

The final stage is 'letting go'. The term 'dis-identify' has been used by some theorists to describe this process of letting go of, and transcending, the former interpretation of 'self'. This is when you move on and no longer look back over your shoulder at how you used to be. This is the new 'you' and you just get on with getting on.

Each person travels the transitional path in their own way and at their own pace. Each person also experiences the distinct subtleties and undercurrents that are relevant to them personally. This is not to say that the stages are not common in most people's experience, it's just that the landscape at each stage may look a little different.

It might be helpful to view this staged model as a roadmap complete with signposts, hazard warnings and a description of the terrain. The map helps make sense of a journey but it is not the journey; it is merely a guide.

Below you'll find a map of the stages. The curved line denotes the emotional ups and downs of the journey.

Try to plot your current position on the curve.

Stage 1	Stage 2	Stage 3	Stage 4	Stage 5	Stage 6	Stage 7	Stage 8	Stage 9
Ignorance is bliss!	Trigger	Revelation	Disintegrating	Finding your voice and being heard	Making sense of it all	Controlling	Integrating	Letting go
Doing what you've always done. Getting what you've always got! People giving you feedback and you not really listening—although you might wonder why people keep telling you the same thing over and over again! Living your usual life pattern, perpetuating your usual approach and style	Something happens to give you a wake up call –the last straw! You experience an undesirable effect to your general approach. You find yourself cornered and feel that you can't escape facing a particular behavioural preference that you possess. You have a shock or enter a crisis	The dawning of the truth; the 'ah ha' moment when you begin to see the effects of your behavioural style and the reason why you're in the place you're in. Looking back, you see the relationship between the way you are and the experiences you have. You begin to see that you are the arbiter of your own fortunes, and they need to change!	Feeling de-skilled and confused. Things that used to work no longer serve you. Wondering what's happening. All the things that have helped you up until now are no longer serving you. Your talents evade you and you may feel distressed or despairing. You feel that things are falling apart	Being able to speak about what you're experiencing and what you want. Finding a sympathetic ear to support you. Hearing yourself talk about things helps make them concrete and manageable. Finding others who have been through a similar experience to you and valuing their support and understanding	Making connections that are meaningful and developing a new frame of reference. Seeing the patterns and linkages in your behaviours and understanding where they've come from and how they do/ dontserve you. Thinking about different approaches that you could develop, authentically, that will help you go forward in the way that you choose. Building new relationships	Managing relationships according to your own values and beliefs and not subjecting yourself to others' control. Controlling your own boundaries. Making conscious choices. Stepping out with a newfound feeing of being in charge of your own interactions and life choices	Gaining a new sense of self. Feeling more complete and more self-determining. Finding that your present experiences and new relationships start connecting up to reinforce your choices. Developing confidence and feeling good about life. Seeing the world in a new light. Taking responsibility for yourself	Seeing things from a different perspective. No longer identifying with the past. Focusing on the future/ Feeling positive and joyous. Feeling powerful and in control. Seeing your past experiences from a 'safe' distance. Perhaps even wondering if you're that same person!

Here is a list of resources to help you move through each stage of the process.

STAGE 1 – IGNORANCE IS BLISS!

Enjoy it!

STAGE 2 – TRIGGER

There's not much you can do about this. It happens.

STAGE 3 – REVELATION

This is the point of dawning. It is a time when you reflect on your past behaviours and begin to see how you have been party to creating the experiences you've had.

Useful activities could be:

▶ Ask a trusted friend for their perception, some feedback and some ideas about what you could have done differently.

▶ Reflect on the dynamics of your communication with those close to you. Ask yourself: What's the usual pattern? What starts the exchange? What happens next? What's the usual outcome? How do you feel about this? (This is a subjective reflection.)

▶ Observe others who are locked into similar patterns of communication (This is an objective reflection.)

▶ Write down your observations. They will be useful markers when you emerge from the process.

STAGE 4 – DISINTEGRATING

You may feel like you're falling apart – but let's not be dramatic!

You can't make an omelette without cracking eggs – as the saying goes. And you can't change yourself without throwing off the old and bringing in the new. Some people think they're losing themselves and, in a sense, they are. Rather as a snake sloughs off its old skin to reveal the new, you are sloughing off old behaviours in order to reveal more of yourself. This can be all absorbing but whilst this is happening, there are some things you can do to help yourself.

Useful activities could be:

▶ Find others who have been through a similar experience and ask them how they negotiated their way through it. They will provide an anchor for you.

▶ Seek professional help to accompany through your process. This will provide some continuity as you complete your 'turning circle'.

▶ Put something nice on your horizon; something rewarding to look forward to.

▶ Engage in familiar activities that you love – music, walking, going to the gym, art, craft, cinema, theatre, reading ... The list is endless. Do anything to get out of your own way and make room for your subconscious mind to exercise its wisdom.

STAGE 5 – FINDING YOUR VOICE AND BEING HEARD

Speaking out has been found to be an effective way to tap one's inner knowledge and learn new things, particularly for women. This is not just about reporting on things as you experience them, it's about empowering yourself to enter a larger conversation with others. These may be others who a like you and sharing similar experiences, or they may be those who are confused by you, or even opposed to you. This is the first time you start to anchor yourself in your new way of being through a new way of communicating.

Useful activities could be:

► Join a support group – or a discussion group – where you can speak your mind and say (and hear) what you think.

► You may have friends or family who are bewildered by your quest to be more assertive. Have a conversation with them to share your experiences and intentions. Not in an apologetic way, but to give them an opportunity to understand and support you.

► Find a 'buddy' who will fall in step with you for a while. (This could be a reciprocal arrangement.)

STAGE 6 – MAKING SENSE OF IT ALL

You'll probably be doing a lot of processing in your mind to try to identify where your behavioural traits have come from and why they have manifested in you in the way that they have. You may find yourself feeling quite frustrated with people who have played a particular role in your past. Try not to be trigger happy with your frustrations and wade in to a confrontation. Indeed, your frustration is as likely, if not more likely, to be with yourself as it is to be with them. Disentangle from your projections onto others and keep your processing personal. This is not about blame and 'if only'. It's about what you're going to do in the future. Stay focused and stay practical using confrontations as a last, and well thought through, resort.

Useful activities could be:

► Take time to reflect (without blaming yourself – or anyone else!) on what caused you to behave in the ways that you did.

► Read books, journals and articles that resonate with your experiences.

► Gather information from wherever you can – family history, personality theory, consultations, support groups ....

► Undertake research into areas related to your own history.

STAGE 7 – CONTROLLING

This is the stage where you'll be making choices about how you manage your boundaries. You'll be asking yourself: 'Who's in?' and 'Who's out?' You'll also be thinking about the basis on which you'll go forward in your relationships and reflecting on the kind of life you want to lead.

Try not to be over-zealous in your newfound freedom of expression. This can be a real turn-off for those who have watched you grow. However, do be true to yourself and make your decisions believing the best of yourself.

▶ Think about your network. Is it time to 'prune' some people? Is it time to introduce yourself to a new circle?

▶ Make some decisions about how you want to move forward in your life – professionally and personally.

▶ Say what you need to say to release yourself from destructive relationships.

▶ Plan to do something that you've always wanted to do. Perhaps you harbour an, as yet, unrealized ambition?

STAGE 8 – INTEGRATING

At a time when you're bringing it all back together, you'll probably be feeling that you've been through quite a transition. This is a time to appraise your values and beliefs and to begin to embody and exemplify the new behaviours that you've unearthed in yourself. It is important that you authentic and more able to express yourself fully. This is not about trying to be something that you're not. You will know, in your heart, what's true for you and what's not. Listen to this part of yourself.

Useful activities could be:

▶ Check into your sense of 'self' to make sure you're expressing it authentically.

▶ Examine your choices to ensure that you're making them as consciously as possible.

▶ Slow things down a little so that you can remember your decisions about how you're going to behave and communicate.

▶ Be conscious of the journey you've been on and go back to your original journal to measure the distance.

STAGE 9 – LETTING GO

Letting go is about shaking the dust from your shoes and going forward unencumbered by the past. This means distinguishing yourself now from how you used to be. It may mean letting go of old animosities and the 'it's not fair' projections onto people from your past. This is characterful stuff and, although simple, it is not easy. However, think about those who hang on to their fury and bitterness and ask yourself if you want to mirror their lives.

Useful activities could be:

▶ Think about your future goals and desires.

▶ Forgive those who have hurt you in the past.

▶ Seize new opportunities and go on new adventures.

▶ Put yourself in the world and meet new people.

▶ Enjoy being confident and determining your own future.

Transitions are different for everyone. Sometimes they are short lived. Sometimes they last for years. Don't rush the process. It has its own rhythm and, although you may go back and forth as you travel through the stages, it will pace you wisely. (Or, rather, you will be pacing yourself wisely, even if you don't realize it!) Opposite is a template to help you capture the ups and downs of your transition: (you may need to transfer it to a larger sheet!)

By understanding how you move through transition and change, you can resource yourself when you next encounter a trigger that sends you into a transition. It will also help you assist others as you will recognize the ups and downs of this process and begin to trust it to point you towards a new horizon.

Record your transition

	Stage 1	Stage 2	Stage 3	Stage 4	Stage 5	Stage 6	Stage 7	Stage 8	Stage 9
This is my experience									
This is how I view my experience									
This is what I'd like to do differently									
This is what I need to learn									
This is how I'm going to learn									
This is the outcome of my experience									

Summary

Transition and change is notoriously difficult to deal with, for many. It can be better understood if it is conceived as a loss, for which there is a grieving period. We have probably all experienced that feeling of hopelessness as we have to let go of something, or someone, and readjust to the world. At whatever level we experience it, whether it be a loss at a deeply personal level or an adjustment to a new professional role, the rhythm is the same; it goes from steady state to chaos to a new steady state. It is the bit in the middle, the chaos, that tends to cause all the trouble because it's all about letting go and trusting your ingenuity to help you find a way through.

This was the final piece of the jigsaw into developing assertiveness skills. Now, having almost completed the workbook, you should be pretty familiar with the intricacies of the topic. But, before you go, there's just one more thing to do – test yourself!

Where to next?

In the final chapter, there is a list of statements which may be allocated to one of the four camps of assertive, aggressive, passive and passive-aggressive. Your task is to make a judgement about which one belongs where.

What have I learnt?

→ How comfortable am I when I encounter change and move through transition?

_____

_____

_____

_____

_____

_____

_____

→ What transitional challenges am I currently facing and how will I approach these?

_____

_____

_____

_____

_____

_____

_____

→ Which stage of moving through change do I find most difficult and why is this so?

_____

_____

_____

_____

_____

_____

_____

_____

→ What resources and support do I need to ensure I embrace change productively?

_____

_____

_____

_____

_____

_____

_____

_____

13 *The final test!*

THIS IS THE FINAL TEST

You have now come to the end of this workbook so you should be fully conversant with assertive behaviour and understand the subtleties of its expression.

Before you go, however, try this test to see how you fare. It is designed to explore how well you've grasped the essence of self-assertion.

In the statements below, a level of assertiveness has been achieved because the people making them have chosen their preferred approach and are honouring it. However, looking beneath the surface, at the 'spirit' of self-assertion, there may be different motivations – self preservation, manipulation, punishment, domination. ...!

Answer 'true' or 'false' to whether the following statements are assertive or not.

	Statement	True ✓	False ✓
1.	'If I don't like what someone is saying, I try to re-direct the conversation. If it doesn't work, I look for an opportunity to make my apologies and leave.'		
2.	'I don't like networking because I think it is self-serving and manipulative.'		
3.	'I dislike bad feelings so I try to get on with most people most of the time, even if I don't like them.'		
4.	'When I listen to a new idea, I tend to look for the flaws in it and debate each one. It's up to the person with the idea to convince me it's good!'		
5.	'If I feel under pressure, I'll ask for some time out so that I can gather my wits around me.'		
6.	'When I'm saying 'No!' to someone's request, I don't give an excuse or an explanation.'		
7.	'I don't always complain because I generally feel able to assert my rights.'		
8.	'I try to agree to others' requests to avoid confrontation.'		
9.	'Although I am known to be a 'people pleaser', I generally get my own way in the end.'		
10.	'I am known for being forthright because I'm happy to tell people what I think.'		
11.	'I try to avoid conflict by being pleasant but if it won't go away, I will make sure I resolve it later."		
12.	'I tend not to invest in what others think and believe, although I'm happy to debate our respective points of view.'		
13.	'I always satisfy my rights!'		

Here are some comments to challenge you to think beneath the surface.

1 **False.** This is not an assertive statement. It is *passive-aggressive*. Indeed, it is a statement made by someone who is reluctant to listen with curiosity (they have already decided that they don't like what's being said) or take responsibility for what they think (at least, overtly.) They have two tactics. The first is an attempt at distraction. The second is withdrawal – or punishment – in the sense that 'if you don't say things I like, I'm leaving!' The person with whom the conversation is taking place may not know what went on or what went wrong. However, the person making the statement will probably feel that they've preserved social niceties by avoiding a, possibly, contentious conversation.

2 **False.** This is not assertive because the person making it has taken themselves out of the frame. It is therefore *passive*. Networking is only manipulative if the intentions of the networker are to get something from someone who might not otherwise be inclined to give it to them. Networking is a reciprocal activity where two people can exchange information or assistance beneficially. It does not thrive on exploitation. In fact, as soon as this is discovered, the networking potential disappears.

3 **False.** This is a *passive* statement. It smacks of falsehood and it suggests that others are incapable of negotiating a more honest relationship around differences in outlook. The person making the statement may feel that they are being kindly by preserving the sensibilities of someone they don't warm to but they are denying them the opportunity to have a more meaningful dialogue.

4 **False.** This is an *aggressive* statement. The reason for this is that they are listening *against* the other

and taking a somewhat inflated view of their own importance in judging the 'rightness' of someone else's thinking.

5 **True.** This is an *assertive* statement. By being able to take time for themselves whilst they think things through they are meeting their needs and preparing to represent themselves honestly. Being assertive does not necessitate an instant response. It is quite OK to ask for time and space to consider a response.

6 **True.** This is an *assertive* statement. Although it sounds a little uncompromising, if you give people apologies, explanations or excuses for saying 'No!' they will try to reason them away leaving you defenceless. It is much harder to justify saying 'No!' if someone demolishes your arguments one by one.

7 **True.** This is an *assertive* statement that suggests the person making it is choosing when it's important to complain and when it is not. If they felt unable to complain ever, it would be a different story but part of being assertive is having the right to choose which battles to fight and which to leave. Being assertive does not mean you have to assert yourself relentlessly.

8 **False.** This is not assertive. It is *passive*. This statement suggests the person making it has a strategy of ingratiation that ensures there are no ripples in any relationships. The trouble is, they'll end up doing everyone else's work for them until they explode! If you don't stop people from breaching boundaries, people will trespass on your capabilities and intrinsic good nature.

9 **False.** This is a *passive-aggressive* statement. What's seen on the outside is not mirrored on the inside. People will experience this person as being co-operative and doing what they can to win favour. The 'punishment' is that they will find a way of meeting their own needs covertly in a Pyrrhic victory, perhaps.

10 **False**. Perhaps. This statement sounds *aggressive* but it may be *assertive* in the sense that they're happy to represent their views **and** hear and take account of others' views too. Alternatively, they may just like imposing their own views on people. It is not clear which communication style this statement is coming from.

11 **True or False.** This statement is a little ambiguous, although, on first reading, it sounds a little *passive-aggressive*. To give it a more *assertive* spin, it might be being made by someone who gives the benefit of the doubt to the other but is not afraid to meet them in opposition if necessary. To take a less flattering view, it might be being made by someone who is trying to bluff a friendly demeanour but is quite capable of coming back to fight their corner, aggressively, if necessary.

12 **True.** This is an *assertive* statement. Although it may come across as disinterested in others' views, it shows that this person is able to 'bracket' these and not get drawn into a 'who's right' and 'who's wrong' argument. Instead, they are showing respect for the other's right to think what they wish whilst, at the same time, respecting their own right to express a contrary view, if they wish to do so.

13 **True** – but with caution. Being assertive is definitely about ensuring your rights are met but if you *always* get your rights met, you must be doing so at the expense of others' rights? Perhaps a proviso should be added to this statement to stop it from becoming aggressive. Something like: 'I always respect my rights but don't always exercise them.'

How did you do?

You may have debated these statements differently, which is good. The point is that it is the spirit of assertiveness that eventually wins the day and not just technique – although technique both underpins and supports assertive behaviour. Being assertive on the 'outside' is necessary but not sufficient to define you as an assertive person. Being assertive on the 'inside' allows you more flexibility in how you wield the tools and techniques of assertion and enables you to pick and choose what works for you at any moment.

Having come full circle, you are now endowed with everything you need to be fully assertive. Hopefully, by now, you will have reversed a dependency and, rather than situations (or people) managing you, you are able to manage them.

Good luck!

Appendix: Resources

TASK SHEET

Looking over the landscape of your learning from your current vantage point, what do you see?

I believe my strongest attributes are:

1. _____

_____

2. _____

_____

3. _____

_____

And my development needs are:

1. _____

_____

2. _____

_____

3. _____

_____

(I must check with a trusted friend that I have drawn appropriate conclusions about myself.)

I have a clear idea about what I want to achieve and there are a number of elements that I need to test out. They are:

1. _____

_____

2. _____

_____

3. _____

_____

The information, assistance and/or skills I need to get me going are:

1. _____

_____

2. _____

_____

3. _____

_____

RESOURCES/SUPPORT

There are some resources/support that I need. This is how and when I will access them:

Resources/Support: I will access these by (activity): I will have them in place by (date):

1. _____

_____

_____

_____

2. _____

_____

_____

_____

3. _____

_____

_____

_____

ACTION PLAN

I am going to commit to the following initial actions, which will be completed by:

Action: *Completion Date:*

1. _____

_____

_____

_____

2. _____

_____

_____

3. _____

_____

_____

_____

QUICK TIPS FOR EMERGENCIES!

If you find yourself coming 'undone' and racked with doubt, pick an idea from the following list to get you back on track again:

- ▶ Remember the good times!
- ▶ Seek more time! Breathe and come back to the issue later when you've had a chance to think about things.
- ▶ Focus on your goals and put the immediate difficulty into a larger context.
- ▶ Step back and imagine what things look like from someone else's vantage point.
- ▶ Distract/forgive yourself by doing something nice.
- ▶ Find a different way of looking at things. Ask yourself 'What else could be going on here?' – Reframe it!
- ▶ Ask yourself 'What assumption am I making about this person/situation?' Your beliefs may be getting in your way.
- ▶ Give feedback. Let people know what's going on for you.
- ▶ Ask a good question to reveal more about the dynamic you're in.
- ▶ Write down all your attributes and the positive comments people make about you.
- ▶ Make a list your successes and unique achievements.
- ▶ Imagine yourself two years from now and think about all the things you have achieved.
- ▶ Listen with genuine curiosity to see if you can fathom different information or motivations.
- ▶ Remember other people don't always get it right – be discerning.
- ▶ Make your choices consciously. (Even if you decide *not* to do something!)
- ▶ Take responsibility for your own well-being – and be kind to yourself.

- ▶ Ask for what you need.
- ▶ Believe the best of yourself.
- ▶ Talk to someone who loves you.
- ▶ Phone a friend!

Bibliography

CHAPTER 1

Honey, P. and Mumford, A. (2000) *The learning styles helper's guide*. Maidenhead: Peter Honey Publications Limited.

Kolb, D.A. (1984) *Experiential learning: experience as the source of learning and development*. Englewood Cliffs, NJ: Prentice Hall.

CHAPTER 2

Berne, Eric (1961) *Transactional Analysis in Psychotherapy*. New York: Grove Press, Inc.,

Ernst, F.H. Jr., M.D. (1971) 'The OK Corral: Grid for Get-On-With', *Transactional Analysis Journal 1:4*, pp1231-240, October.

CHAPTER 9

Adapted from Senge, Peter M., Jaworski, Joseph, Scharmer, C. Otto and Flowers, Betty Sue (2005) *Presence: Exploring Profound Change in People, Organisations and Society*

CHAPTER 12

Maslow, A. H. (1968, 1999) *Toward a Psychology of Being*, pp 106–107, John Wiley & Sons, Inc

Michelli, Georgina (Dena) (2004), 'A Grounded Theory Study of Adults' Experiences of Transformative Learning as part of Personal Development', PhD thesis, University of Surrey

Index

Notes

Notes

Notes

Notes